THE MISTRESS MANUAL

The Good Girl's Guide to Female Dominance

by Mistress Lorelei

greenery press

Published in the United States by Greenery Press, 1447 Park Ave., Emeryville, CA 94608.

www.greenerypress.com

ISBN 978-1-890159-19-1

TABLE OF CONTENTS

INTRODUCTION:
How to Use The Mistress Manual

*"Most power is illusory and perceptual. You have to create an environment
in which people perceive you as having some power." – Carrie Saxon Perry*

Being a Domme is as much a matter of attitude as actions. The ideas you
will find here are not an inflexible etiquette, a single violation of which will
disqualify you from the sisterhood, but an infinitely variable recipe for enjoying
sensual dominance. For some of you, that dominance will be a delightful bedroom
game; for others, it will become the basis for a whole new way of handling
relationships.

I can't tell you exactly what will please you sexually. What I can offer is
practical suggestions, safety tips, and insights into guysub psychology, plus
something to do with your hands while you figure out what you like.

One thing I hope I can do here is help you understand and accept that it's
okay to want sexual power – or any other kind of power, come to think of it.
Although I've been thinking kinky thoughts and doing kinky things for most of
my life, I encountered the same kinds of struggles in coming to self-acceptance as
many Dommes.

Perhaps most important, "The Mistress Manual" is the work, not of a
submissive male fantasizing about the perfect Dominatrix, but by a practicing
Mistress herself, with the help and advice of various friends who also believe in
maintaining a firm hand on the reins. I am not a professional Dominatrix, but a
happy amateur with years of experience in controlling a stubborn male submissive. (Although that phrase may sound to an inexperienced Mistress like a
contradiction in terms, I assure you it is not. If submissive males were always

compliant, the Mistress's task would be considerably simpler – but possibly less fun. But more of that later.) What you'll get here is what, in my considerable experience, actually works.

What Is a Mistress?

To the vulgar-minded person a Mistress is a male's sexual plaything, pathetically eager to please the arrogant male who financially supports her, dropping every other interest (if she has any) to be at his beck and call for an afternoon tryst. In short, she is not Mistress; he is Master.

How different is our conception of a Mistress! She crooks her little finger, and her male submissive rushes to obey. She declares her displeasure in no uncertain terms, and her vassal quivers in fright, knowing that his inevitable punishment will be severe. She lounges at her ease, and her sissy maid serves her, curtsying as he proffers a tray. She is strong, cruel, in command; he is powerless, punished, in submission. Yet both are happy, far happier, I daresay, than the other sort of Mistress and her keeper.

The Mistress draws her ideas and fantasies from a broad range of possibilities. There are five basic fantasy archetypes, but (since you're the Domme), you don't have to adhere to any one of them. The patterns are, in fact, the basic male fantasies. It's helpful to understand them, but you need not feel bound by them. You can choose the activities and attitudes you like from any of these roles – and yes, it is possible to do the kind of heavy leather scene an Amazon enjoys, but with the tenderness of a Nursemaid.

1. *The affectionate Nursemaid,* who teases, clysters, and chastises her diapered charge.

2. *The stern Governess,* who spanks, paddles, and canes a naughty schoolboy.

3. *The harsh and exacting Queen,* who demands constant service and punishes her sissy maid.

4. *The cruel Amazon,* who mocks, dominates, and torments her sex slave.

5. *The Goddess,* who commands worship of her female beauty and divinity.

There are, of course, other roles in other fantasies, but these five are the basic patterns of most guysub fantasies. (More details on the five types of fantasies – how to identify and use them – is given in Chapter 9.)

As a skilled Mistress, I understand how to employ these roles so as to take advantage of their subtle individual charms. In the pages of "The Mistress Manual," I will train you, my dear Reader, to do so. If you apply yourself to your lessons, you can learn to dominate your man for a lifetime, guaranteeing yourself continuing sexual pleasure and the satisfaction of a job well done. In return, your submissive will offer you slavish devotion, for only in the wise care of a well-trained Mistress can he find peace and happiness.

What Makes This Book Different?

Since the first edition of "The Mistress Manual" came out, a number of how-to books have become available for the eager but inexperienced Domme. Yet this book is still different and valuable. For one thing, it is essentially written from a Domestic Discipline point of view. Although plenty of resources are available for doing great Leather scenes, the Domestic Discipline world by its very nature has had far fewer realistic, down-to-earth discussions of technique. All too often, publications designed to appeal to the Domestic Discipline culture emphasize fantasy at the expense of practical instruction or safety.

Domestic Discipline and Leather are different styles of power-exchange play. (See Table 1 for a detailed comparison of the two styles.) Understanding which style you and your partner prefer is going to have a strong influence on how you approach a scene, what you say, even how you dress. Although there are plenty of overlaps between the styles, finding the attitude that works best for you and your sub can mean the difference between a successful scene and a failure.

The Domestic Discipline style is based on psychodrama, the enactment of a sensual ritual where the dramatic structure of the fantasy is just as important as the physical sensations – perhaps more important. This layer of fantasy can give scenes an enormous emotional power. Paradoxically, by distancing the submissive from his ordinary self, he is able to reach deep into his soul and feel things utterly forbidden. Instead of asking for pain directly, the submissive becomes a naughty boy who must be punished. Instead of saying, "I like crossdressing, because it makes me hot," he is forced into ruffles and lace by a cruel Mistress. Of course, both players know that it is all done by consent – but the fantasy of nonconsent is a vital part of the game.

The world within the fantasy looks considerably different from the world outside it. One aspect that sometimes puzzles or offends Leather people and vanilla folk alike is that within the fantasy, all women are Dommes who must be worshipped and all men are naughty boys who must be controlled by a powerful woman.

Domestic Discipline	Leather
Fantasy of nonconsent	Open negotiations
Psychodrama and role-playing	Intensification of self
Fantasy of female supremacy and universal Dommeing	Many orientations and combinations acceptable
Forced Femme	Willing crossdressing
Pain as "punishment"	Pain as pleasure/submission
Punishment implements tend toward traditional spanking toys	Toys ranging from traditional to electrical, floggers, and elaborate equipment
Corner time	Dungeon time
Playful, arch	Serious, wicked
Mostly heterosexual and often sexualized; sometimes FemDomme/femsub, but rarely sexualized	GuyDom and FemDomme styles very similar
Victorian/Fifties style very common	Costume play relatively rare
Collar a useful place to attach a leash	Collar a vital symbol of commitment
Almost entirely a private scene	Play occurs both in private and public
Thinks of itself as a fantasy	Thinks of itself as an aspect of reality
Rarely self-identifies as SM or even BDSM	Proudly BDSM
Can be bedroom or lifestyle	Can be bedroom or lifestyle
Play can be mild or emotionally and physically intense	Play can be mild or emotionally and physically intense

Table 1. Domestic Discipline versus Leather

Yes, there are genuine female supremacists out there, who really believe that males are nasty or helpless or childish and that women are innately superior. But there are many, many more Dommes who play with that idea during scene and put it away afterward.

Although Leather has its rituals and roles as well, there is a tough core of honesty in it. Submissives may sometimes be punished with pain, but more often they are beaten because the Mistress wants to beat them – and because they like it, even though it hurts. The raw emotional power of Dominance and submission, sadism and masochism – without frills, with only a few chosen rituals – is also enormous. But it appeals in a different way from Domestic Discipline's cozy roleplay.

Domestic Discipline and Leather are also communities of kinky people. Although what they do is similar enough to create some overlap, it's also just different enough in style and attitude that there is sometimes a regrettable amount of hostility between the two camps. Leather people sometimes fail to see beyond the lace and flowers and fantasies and dismiss Domestic Discipline people as "not real players" whose BDSM activities are insufficiently intense or honest. (They have never seen a classic Domestic Discipline caning, which may leave weals for two or three weeks.) Some Domestic Discipline people look with scorn or fear at Leather people, whose style may be threatening but who are, in my experience, loving and gentle as well as fierce.

I cannot, singlehanded, reconcile the two communities. I came out of the Domestic Discipline community and now belong to the Leather world, and I have friends in both camps. What I can do is make it clear that both are to be respected – and that in this book, if I speak with the voice of a Domestic Discipline Goddess, discussing painplay in terms of punishment, I do at least know the difference between that fantasy and reality. The reality is, of course, that I am not a goddess (if I were, the world would be considerably different). What I am – for real, at heart, in scene and out of scene – is a Domme and a Leatherwoman.

Using *The Mistress Manual*

The impatient Reader may sigh, looking at "another great, square, thick book" that demands her attention. You need not read the book straight through, as though it were a text assigned for class. Instead, browse through the table of contents, seeking topics that interest you. Make notes to yourself about which techniques seem exciting.

You may choose to allow your sub, as a special treat, to read a section or two of the book, but I strongly recommend that you do not permit him to read the whole book. Revealing a Mistress's secrets is prejudicial to the maintenance of order, and if possible you should avoid using harsh measures to re-establish your authority. (Frankly, it isn't good form. A steady authority combined with a capricious taste in chastisements is not only more effective, it's better style.)

Moreover, your submissive will gain far more true satisfaction from a new and surprising punishment – especially if he believes you have created it just for him – than from any exercise from a book. Later on, however, when the punishment is more familiar, you should use anticipation to intensify his sensations. All things in their time!

Instead of sharing the book with your submissive, why not discuss it with a friend who also enjoys Female Dominance? If you are unsure of her tastes, it could provide an effective opening for the discussion of your habits and fantasies. If you know her to be a Mistress, reading the book together could spark fascinating discussions of theory and practice, in which you both could learn new ideas. Few people need a support system as much as the Mistress; her entire existence is a rebellion against our patriarchal culture, and despite her strength, her isolation calls for the help and encouragement of her Dominant sisters.

Part I: Becoming a Mistress

Becoming a Mistress – whether that means taking up sexual power, lifestyle power, or both – can be a challenge. Although some lucky young girls have never lost their magical sense of their own power and glory, too many women have had the authority crushed out of them at an early age. This section of *The Mistress Manual* will guide you through the process of claiming your feminine authority and entering the world of female domination.

Chapter 1 is a catalogue raisonée of the many exquisite pleasures proper to dominant women and their male submissives. Experienced ladies will be refreshed by the listing, while girls new to the game will begin to understand the attractions of petticoat government not just for themselves, but also for their subservient partners.

Chapter 2 is designed for the reluctant Dominatrix: a woman who fears to take up her scepter and call her Queendom her own. Her partner may ardently desire to humble his male self at her feet, yet she resists. In this chapter I offer some suggestions to convince the guilty or unwilling Mistress to give female rule a try. In addition, I include a brief philosophical justification for female rule that should encourage even the most egalitarian young lady.

Chapter 3 addresses another problem: that of the Dominatrix with no slave to serve her. How can she persuade the macho man of her heart to surrender to her authority or, failing that, find a submissive male? These vexing questions are answered in frank detail.

Chapter 4 offers some useful advice on maintaining a healthy relationship while practicing female domination. Although most couples have no problems adjusting to a feminine regime (especially a part-time one), some do encounter difficulties. I list the warning signs of trouble and make some suggestions for keeping your relationship strong and healthy.

Part II: The Mistress in Action

This section of *The Mistress Manual* is a primer for your delightful first steps into the practice of female dominance. Experienced Mistresses may smile at some of the basic material I include, but even the most formidable females had to begin her career somewhere.

Chapter 5 offers techniques for making the session thoroughly engaging and fulfilling. From the vital issue of pain versus suspense, to the role of body language in female dominance, this chapter covers all the basic ideas you need to understand before you plan an actual scene.

Chapter 6 gives a guided tour of how to plan, structure, and conduct that most stimulating of games, the session. Instead of giving you an unvarying script to follow – ultimately, I fear, a very dull proceeding, allowing no scope to your own rich imagination – I have outlined for you the necessary steps in the design of your own fantasy session, unique, individual, and ultimately satisfying. For additional ideas and suggestions, you may turn to the riches of Part III.

Chapter 7 is a treatise on the delightful art of disciplining naughty male submissives, from the simple (yet effective) over-the-knee hand spanking to the elaborate and erotic rituals of birching. Each instrument, style, and technique is discussed in glowing detail.

Chapter 8 covers the various other skills a Mistress needs to Dominate her submissive male in every circumstance, including a most illuminating section on achieving her own pleasure while continuing to keep her slave in tight control.

Part III: The Five Archetypal Fantasies

The six chapters in this section discuss the subject of fantasy: what it is, how it works, how to understand and enjoy your submissive's fantasies and your own.

The archetypal structure given here is a useful convenience, not a Mistress's command engraved in stone. Although most submissives have a major fantasy that falls into one of the five archetypes, they also have a minor fantasy from one of the other archetypes, and may even combine elements from several of the basic fantasies. So you should read all the chapters and adapt the techniques for your male's fantasy. If your vassal is a sissy maid, for example, he may not be interested in diapering per se, but he may enjoy the occasional humiliation of being dressed as an infant for punishment.

To begin, peruse Chapter 9 and decide which fantasy archetype most appeals to you. Then read the chapter in which the archetype is explained. You will find detailed information on the elements of the fantasy and specific hints on script, costume, setting, and props. I also reveal the skills you must develop to become an effective Mistress, including detailed discussions of various levels and techniques of play, and a delineation of the needs of your submissive in each situation. (As you may imagine, an Amazon's slave has a very different set of needs, desires, and appropriate behaviors than a naughty schoolboy or a sissy maid!)

I then walk you, step by step, through a sample fantasy session, giving hints on what you and your submissive will be feeling and doing at each stage; how, when, and why to start the session; potential problems in the scene; and how to finish the scene in grand style.

After you have found your fantasy and read up on it, browse through the other chapters, even those that least appeal to you. You may find unexpected treasures. If you are a natural Amazon, you may never have given a thought to the use of enemas, although you probably use butt plugs and other anal stimulation. Yet the instructions on careful administration of an enema can be readily adapted to your style, simply by altering the dialogue and changing the reason for using the technique (from punishing naughty thoughts to thoroughly cleansing a newly purchased slave, for example).

Having claimed your authority and your power, you now have an abundance of ideas and techniques for exerting them. Enjoy the process. Your submissive certainly will.

Assumptions and Received ideas

In this volume I have made several assumptions. In order to avoid the ennui of repeating certain warnings over and over again, let me state here that I am assuming that the two of you are involved in a lasting, monogamous relationship (whether that is friendship or marriage or something between is up to you); that neither of you is HIV-positive or that both of you are; that you are otherwise physically healthy and normal; that you are consenting adults, not kidnap victims or children; that you are not seeking to harm one another emotionally or in any other sense; that you are reasonable and stable human beings; that you do not include third parties (or fourth, or eightieth) in your games without their full knowledge and informed consent; that you are using Female Dominance as a fantasy or lifestyle mutually agreed upon and agreeable.

I am not responsible – legally, morally, or in any other fashion – for the mental, emotional, moral, or physical well-being of any reader who contravenes these rules, behaves irresponsibly, misreads instructions, suffers physical or emotional traumas, or has physical or emotional problems apparently arising from participation in fantasy play. In other words, you are grown-ups now, and fully responsible for your own safety and health. Should you harm yourself or someone else during play, the fault is entirely and legally your own. Clear? Now you can begin to have fun.

Part One

BECOMING A MISTRESS

1

WHY BECOME A MISTRESS?:
Some Unexpected Pleasures

*"When we are flat on our backs there is no way to look but up." – Roger W.
Babson*

For my readers who have already tasted the heady wine of total control over
a submissive male, this question may seem absurd. The answer is so obvious:
being a Mistress is fun. Female Dominance offers the Mistress a cornucopia of
delights. (The submissive male enjoys it too, although there are moments in scene
when he may not seem to do so.)

But why should a woman enjoy forcing her beloved husband into a
humiliating costume of corset, high heels, and ruffled sissy panties? What would
make a man, often a powerful, highly paid professional, gladly submit to a severe
spanking while so attired? What is so much fun about playing power games?

The reasons generally fall into three categories. First, the joy of escape into
a fantasy world. Second, the sheer sensual delight of the costumes, the risk, and
the physical stimulation. Third, the bliss of sharing the deepest possible intimacy
and trust with another human being.

The Joy of Fantasy. No matter how pleasant and fulfilling your daily life is,
sometimes you need to escape from your role as responsible adult, dutiful worker,
or dedicated family member. The more stressful that role is, the further it is from
your own deepest impulses, the more you need an escape from the limitations of
everyday life. Some people use alcohol, drugs, or gambling to transcend their
ordinary lives, but these activities generally prove to be both destructive and
unsatisfying. But the escape provided by a rich fantasy life can be constructive and

extraordinarily fulfilling. Instead of destroying true intimacy, shared fantasy increases it. Instead of harming the body, sexual release helps it. Instead of stifling the needs of your true self, fantasy allows you to express and realize your deepest needs – and in the process, fantasy brings forth a new, stronger reality.

A New and Powerful Self. The practice of Female Domination allows the Mistress to express her power, the tough and controlling part of herself that may be unacceptable at work or in the community. When you assume the role of Mistress, with its attendant garb, behavior, speech, and rituals, you may feel like you are becoming someone else. In the process, you will find yourself allowed to say and do things strictly forbidden in ordinary life. Paradoxically, that someone else is yourself – just a part of yourself that you don't ordinarily allow to speak.

The transformation is uniquely liberating. Letting your wicked and powerful inner self out to play is more than a sure cure for stress. In Jungian terms, it is a way of integrating your Shadow, the hidden and rejected self.

Becoming a Dominatrix may at first seem schizophrenic, especially if you are still a nice girl. Later you will find the Mistress's powers infiltrating your daily life. For example, you may become more assertive in ordinary situations. If you can imagine commanding your leering male boss to lick your shoes for daring to take a liberty with you, you may react with the proper icy disdain (plus lawsuit) when he sexually harasses you, instead of asking yourself what you did to invite his unspeakable caresses. Eventually your Dominatrix self will be, not the opposite of your usual self, but a playful intensification of it.

As a Mistress, you will be able to command the respect you may not otherwise receive, because on many levels, our culture devalues the female and exalts the male. Every day women suffer the onslaughts of power-maddened males, from rowdy construction workers to condescending bankers. (Congress alone should turn any self-respecting woman into a Dominatrix.) It is a positive pleasure to come home from an encounter with a stupid, crude, or demeaning male to a sissy maid who worships and adores your divine femaleness. A properly trained male submissive will respect all the attributes of the female, from our pedicured feet to our delicate panties to our beautiful hair. And yes – our power as well.

Moreover, you will enjoy the thrill of rebelling against all the deluded creatures (male and female) who taught you that men must be placated, appeased, and served. As a Mistress, you will order a male to placate, appease, and serve you, a welcome change.

There is also the simple excitement of power, which has been called the greatest aphrodisiac. Having your commands obeyed, your womanhood worshipped, and your lightest wishes treated as urgent commands is extremely arousing. You will learn to revel in the wicked thrills of power: forcing a man into helpless bondage, ordering him to act as your maid, demanding hours of oral service from his willing mouth and tongue. The infliction of play punishment becomes a thrilling experience, for your blows (which he deserves and desires) will not only produce gratifying evidence of your power in the form of tears, cries, and reddened nether cheeks, they will also produce a change in your partner's behavior. Most of us wish to have an effect in this world, and being a Mistress produces quite entertaining and immediate effects.

A practical pleasure, but one not to be scorned, is the maid service a wise Mistress can extract from her submissive. Most women must beg, nag, and scold their men into doing housework, to no avail. Whether doing housework is part of your submissive's fantasy – and it may well not be – negotiating power play can make negotiating other roles much easier. If you have a sissy maid, your house-cleaning days may well be over, for he takes pleasure in serving. Cooking, housecleaning, laundry (especially delicate hand laundry) can all become part of his sexual satisfaction and evidence of your growing power.

A New and Powerless Self. But what pleasure does the male find in his embarrassing and frequently painful role? He too has a Shadow, a self he cannot acknowledge or express in ordinary life. Boys mustn't cry, or wear frilly clothes, or be passive; they have to be strong, silent, macho men. His role as sissy maid or well-spanked schoolboy or diapered baby permits him to express forbidden emotions and wear taboo clothing. If he simply wants, openly and sincerely, to surrender his will to a woman, that need, as intense and undeniable as thirst, can finally be slaked in scene.

Given society's constant demands on men to be masculine, to take charge, to succeed, to get it up and keep it up, to do instead of be, it is no wonder that some of the strongest, brightest, and most successful males seek contact with their hidden selves through submission to a woman's firm but kindly rule.

The pleasures of the submissive are the polar opposites of (and therefore closely akin to) the pleasures of the Mistress. It is a truism that all polarities express the opposite ends of a single principle or idea. Like yin and yang, darkness and light, submissive male and dominant female need one another to be complete.

Moreover, the two are not simply opposites. Even the most severe Mistress takes pleasure not only in compelling her slave's submission, but also in fulfilling his fantasies. Likewise, the most subservient slave enjoys not only surrendering to his Mistress's power, but also gratifying his own hidden desires. In short, however absolute the lady's command may seem, it is always tempered with a concern for her submissive's satisfaction and well-being. And likewise, however abject a slave may appear, he is in some sense in control of the situation, for if he refused to respond, the Dominatrix would no longer be in charge. The two roles are symbiotic.

Moreover, a submissive never starts out powerless. He must have power in order to hand it over to his Mistress, who holds it in a blind trust until he needs it back. That may be at the end of a scene, after renegotiation, or even at the end of a lifestyle relationship.

Nothing Could Be More Natural. The first power we all know is female. Although not all women are interested in exercising that power as a Mistress, both men and women find a certain innate fitness in female Dominance. It is a return to childhood and the loving rule of our mothers, who might punish but who always forgave.

Although all women start life as daughters, not mothers, they must someday move forward from being a powerless child to being a woman in authority. Becoming a Dominatrix is one way to celebrate your innate female strength. Indeed, every woman, whether she becomes a mother or chooses not to bear children, must experience the transformation into a female authority in order to become an adult and truly her own Mistress. (This is true even of female submissives, who find their greatest joy in surrender; choosing to surrender, choosing their own Dominant, understanding and fulfilling their own sexuality, is a position of genuine power – power surrendered, but nevertheless consciously known, used, felt.)

This transformation was considerably simpler in the days when Goddess worship was the rule. Without taking a stand on any specific form of modern Goddess worship, I must say that when the Feminine face of the Deity is neglected, things go sadly wrong. (See Chapter 2 for more information.) Even without a solid religious structure to help a young girl deal with her passage into womanhood, she must learn to accept and use her innate female power.

Sensual Enjoyments. Aside from the psychological satisfactions outlined above, there are physical pleasures unique to Dominance/submission relationships. The role of Mistress is both demanding and sexually satisfying. The role of submissive – whether maid, slave, schoolboy – can stretch a male to his limits but ends in true, deep release.

Intense Stimulation. The submissive male enjoys female Domination because it feels good. His major reward is erotic pleasure of an exceptionally intense and prolonged nature. Some of the components of that pleasure may not seem too enjoyable – spankings, enemas or diapering, foot worship, cock-and-ball torture – but they are pleasurable, partly because they are so intense, partly because they promote a psychological letting-go that enables a male to achieve a splendid orgasm (if his Mistress permits).

Perhaps the prime sensual enjoyment is the one least explicable to those who have never played the game. Intense stimulation may seem like pain, but it is not (primarily) pain. The deep muscle stimulation of a spanking or paddling; the sense of compression inside a tightly laced corset or a locked male chastity device; the overwhelming feeling of being possessed that comes from anal penetration; the smaller but still intense sensations from the plucking of pubic hairs, the pinching of nipples, or the pricking of the male's glans: all these are intense stimulations. Under their influence, the male forgets himself and his worries, becoming no more than a sexual toy for an all-powerful female tyrant. His mind cannot drift toward work or money or any other mundane consideration. He is bombarded by sensations – some painful, some pleasurable, some mixed, all intense.

Within the world of the fantasy, all these feelings are not only permitted but encouraged. And they are enjoyed at the will of an imperious and often capricious Mistress, so the additional psychological stimulation of suspense is added to the already overpowering physical sensations. Best of all, he is not permitted to spoil the stimulation by reaching orgasm.

The sensation of being simultaneously urged forward and held back, both whipped and curbed, is the great defining experience of male submission. The result is stimulation added to stimulation, multiplied, reduplicated, intensified almost to screaming point. Then the sudden release of orgasm.

Restraint, even forced restraint, increases male sexual satisfaction. Too many men, seeking immediate release, rush through foreplay and intercourse, frustrating their partners and shortchanging themselves. Under the tuition of a Mistress, such males learn that their sexual satisfaction must be delayed until the lady has had her fill of pleasure. A skilled Dominatrix will prolong the male's sexual arousal, simultaneously forbidding and encouraging it, and thereby give him the great gift of true release.

The Dominatrix enjoys prolonged stimulation as well. Both the demonstration of her power and the subduing of her slave are quite arousing, but she often (if she is wise) has another form of pleasure available to her. (And it's good for her partner as well.) I refer to the ancient and sacred practice of cunnilingus. Few women can get enough of this luscious activity, while submissive males find it the ultimate act of worship. It fulfills the twin criteria of intensity and restraint, for the male submissive kneeling before his lady's Shrine is overpowered by his nearness to her most intimate secrets. Nevertheless, he cannot mar the experience by climaxing too rapidly, especially if the Mistress has had the forethought to fasten him into a secure chastity device. (See Chapter 8 for an illuminating discussion of ways to maintain control of your submissive male while you are close to swooning with your fifth orgasm.)

The Freedom to Feel. Paradoxically, many people find Dominance and submission fantasies liberating. Under the feigned duress lies real permission to let go and enjoy acts, clothes, or sensations that are otherwise strictly forbidden. Moreover, the submissive need feel no guilt for enjoying these things; not only did his cruel Mistress force him into those ruffled panties or that demeaning position of servitude, she also "punished" him for his transgression. The scenario of misbehavior, punishment, and forgiveness is a classic Aristotelian plot that offers both actors their traditional catharsis.

The submissive's release often includes tears. During Dominance play, many submissives resolve other tensions in their lives. Some males cannot cry except in the context of the game. Others need to express other taboo emotions: fear, anger, rebellion, contrition, or helplessness. After his forbidden outburst, the Mistress punishes him and then offers forgiveness and consolation.

Submissive males, especially those in positions of extraordinary responsibility, also seek respite from the stress of constant decision-making. It's a relief to be told precisely what to do and how to do it, to have the penalties for mistakes so clear-cut and so immediate. A session of schoolboy discipline, for example, may be painful but it is also sure to have a happy ending. Real life is never so well choreographed or so satisfying.

Forbidden Silk and Lace and Leather. Yet another attraction of female Domination is the chance to wear different clothes. Costumes, like uniforms, transform and identify their wearers. For the submissive male, who must wear tailored suits and strangling neckties to work, a maid's uniform or a small boy's clothing represent a break with the grind of daily life and an escape into the freedom of a new self.

Many male submissives enjoy dressing in women's clothing. Female garb is the ultimate break with society's standards for manhood: deeply shaming, for every male is raised to despise the sissy, yet also compellingly erotic. Women's clothing, with its soft textures, its lovely colors, its delicate construction, is designed to be sensual. Furthermore, it has the attraction of the utterly taboo. A man in female dress is far beyond the bounds of the acceptable and is therefore free. Lastly, it is associated with women and their mysteries and the sexual bliss they may grant the male. Many males believe (wrongly, God knows) that women's lives are far easier than men's. Is it any wonder that they seek an escape in the clothing and accessories of the blessed female?

Sharing Intimacy and Trust. Without trust, a healthy Dominance/submission relationship is impossible. Only trust allows partners to discuss their fantasies in the first place, much less act them out in great detail. Especially if the fantasy entails servitude, bondage, humiliation, or pain (and what submissive's fantasies do not?), the deepest possible trust is necessary to make the relationship work in the long term. Though some people find it easier to share their sexual secrets with strangers, many others find such trust takes time to build. For them, one-night stands are out of the question. It is impossible to pick a man up, learn his needs, fulfill them and yourself, and then disappear, all within the space of a few hours.

By giving over his body to his Mistress, a submissive male is saying, "I trust you completely." But what does that trust entail?

First, the Mistress is responsible to know and respect her partner's limits. If she stays too far within his bounds, he may feel frustrated, disappointed, and unsatisfied. If she crosses the line too far, he could be hurt, emotionally or physically. Learning how to push a man to his limits – and not beyond – is a complex process, and it takes time.

Nevertheless, once that trust has been established, it is one of the great sources of joy in a relationship. My submissive husband trusts me with his body and knows I will not hurt him more than he needs; he also knows that I am responsive and loving to his more conventional needs, and that he can trust me with his life as well as with a razor, some soap, and his testicles.

Perhaps most important, sharing fantasies deepens the bonds between partners. A submissive man who knows his wife or lover understands his deepest sexual needs (needs he may have always been too ashamed of and too frightened to share) will be contented, faithful, and affectionate. A Dominant Woman who understands her husband's fantasies well enough to construct a satisfying scene for him will also understand other things about him, and she will be strong enough to demand her rights should he attempt to grow domineering in their daily relationship. Marriages in which the Wife is Dominant are often the most egalitarian and the most truly satisfying. Furthermore, the Dominance/submission relationship is often played out as a switch: one time he takes control, the next he does. Such trust and intimacy are bound to help make a very happy marriage.

If you are interested in the step-by-step creation of such intimacy, skip Chapter 2 and go on to Chapter 3. If you still have doubts, read Chapter 2 before you go on.

2

THE RELUCTANT MISTRESS:
Learning to Love Command

How shall I rule over others, that hath not full power and command of myself? – François Rabelais

Despite the catalogue of the pleasures of Female Domination given in Chapter 1, you have turned to this chapter. Therefore I deduce that you are suffering some conflict over your role as Mistress. You may feel guilty or ashamed about your fantasies of Dominating men, or you may be in love with a man who has submissive fantasies and wants you to act them out with him. (He probably gave this book to you, unless, in a valiant effort to learn, you purchased it for yourself.) And you, wishing to please him but unwilling or unable to Rule him, feel lonely, confused, unhappy, repelled, or utterly inadequate. Possibly you yourself are a submissive, and despair at the thought of ever assuming authority.

Is it possible for you to learn to love command? Can you become a happy, effective, and satisfied Mistress? YES! Not every Female Tyrant started life with fantasies of punishing and controlling helpless males. Many learned first how to go through the motions of Dominance play and only later came to enjoy the experience.

Not only will this book teach you how to become a Mistress but also how to have fun doing so. It is scarcely my intention to oppress Women with yet another duty owed to males. If, after listening to my suggestions and giving the fantasy a reasonable trial, you find that you do not enjoy Female Domination, don't do it! If your male still insists, dump him. No one has the right to force you into sexual acts that make you feel uncomfortable. However, you do owe yourself a chance to try to understand and enjoy this new realm of experience. You may find that you enjoy it very much indeed.

If you have long-standing fears or conflicts over sexual issues, do yourself the greatest possible kindness and see a therapist. The process may be painful, but (given a decent therapist and your own willingness to work) it can change your life.

The Repressed Dominatrix

Is it possible to be a Domme and not know it? Absolutely. That's why it's always worth trying. Remember, if you hate it, you don't have to keep doing it.

I've known several wonderful Dommes who managed to go through twenty, thirty, forty years without noticing their own deep need for sexual control. Then something changed – a friend suggested it to them, or they heard or read a story that unleashed their needs. Then all the repressed Dommeliness flowed back into their lives, energizing them sexually and giving new depth and pleasure to their relationships.

Because our families and society don't offer much support or many positive role models for Women who need sexual control, it can be easy for us to pack away our dangerous desires until it's safe to bring them into the light. For years after I became an active Domme, I kept stumbling into memories of old fantasies and old activities that now, in hindsight, seemed unmistakably Domme. The hours and hours I spent on the phone with my best friend when we were fourteen, planning to kidnap a male friend of ours, were a definite clue; the elaborate and dark kidnapping fantasies I had then had been totally repressed and forgotten until a friend asked me for suggestions on doing a consensual kidnapping scene. I'd also forgotten the dungeon fantasies I had dating from my earliest years in school. The games I played with my first lover – making him sit up and beg, roll over, even bark – were so Dommely that I laughed aloud when I remembered them. I was sixteen then, but I had completely forgotten doing it. Being a Domme wasn't emotionally safe for me then, so I saved it for the time when I was strong enough to do it right.

The Guilty Dominatrix

Perhaps you haven't repressed your needs. All your life you have fantasized about Dominating a helpless male. Your dreams may range from (relatively) conventional spanking scenes to fantasies of keeping a male as a sex slave to torment, tease, and control. But you have never gone forth to find a submissive male. Why not? Here are some possible reasons:

1. *You can't respect a man who wants to be Dominated.*

2. *You don't believe any men actually want to be Dominated.*

3. *You're afraid the real experience won't measure up to your fantasies.*

4. *You're afraid that you would or could seriously hurt the submissive male.*

5. *You don't believe that it's morally right for Women to Dominate men.*

6. *Your man (past or current) tried it and hated it. There's no point in trying again.*

I shall deal with these problems one by one, in numbered order.

1. *You can't respect a man who wants to be dominated.* Somewhere inside, you secretly cherish the image of the macho male so celebrated by our patriarchal culture. I could simply dismiss this as an individual aberration (if you haven't noticed that Rambo is a homicidal maniac and an asshole to boot, you're hopeless), except that this widespread attitude must be demolished. Otherwise, strong and healthy Women may find themselves wondering uneasily if their submissive males aren't, well, a little unmanly. Nothing could be further from the truth!

    First, let's take a look at the Rambo model of masculinity. (I could evince a dozen other actors who have made this disgusting creature their specialty, but why advertise them?) His best points are physical strength and willingness to defend his family or his honor (usually the latter). His worst points are a deranged predilection for violence, unveiled hatred and contempt for Women, unwillingness to listen to reason, and total emotional isolation except for an occasional Female bedmate (who is killed off by the end of the film) and his male buddy (and God knows they scarcely share much real feeling, unless committing mass murder together can be called a sharing experience). He doesn't think, read, feel, or talk. He kills. His only emotion is rage, and all too often that rage is turned against Women, who in these films are always either pure good passive Females (almost invariably victims) or slaughterous bitches.

    Is that real manliness? Do you want your sons growing up to behave like that?

    A submissive male, on the other hand, serves, honors, and respects Women. He can feel; the whole point of the fantasy is often to provide an outlet for emotions our society has defined as forbidden to men. His deep emotional connection to his Mistress enables them to share the fantasy.

    But is he strong? Absolutely. He would lay down his life for his Mistress. And he's likely, statistically speaking, to be a high-earning professional, an intellectual, a powerful man with a responsible job. A man who needs the release of letting someone else decide and choose for once; a man who understands that his Feminine side, crushed by the ceaseless demands of his work, must find some expression in his life.

The modern ideal of manhood is based on the machine. No, not just any machine, a machine gun. The submissive male's ideal of manhood is the medieval ideal, a man sworn to serve and protect an all-powerful Lady; he is proud to wear her favor, to show the world the Woman to whom he owes allegiance, love, and service. Though he can fight, he can also love. He is not ashamed of his emotions or his spirituality. He is both a poet and a knight, a complete human being. And he longs with all his heart to serve his Mistress.

Which man is more worth your respect?

2.   *You don't believe any men actually want to be dominated.* Just look in the classifieds of any alternative newspaper. They're begging for it. A man may be too shy to tell you his fantasies on the first date, but just you suggest it and see how fast he'll jump at the chance.

3.   *You're afraid the real experience won't measure up to your fantasies.* Possibly it won't at first. Developing a shared fantasy takes time and trust. Follow the detailed instructions given in subsequent chapters, and you'll have both a healthy relationship and a satisfying role as Mistress. After you've grown used to actually commanding a male, mere fantasy Rule will forever seem flat and pallid to you.

4.   *You're afraid that you would or could seriously hurt your submissive male.* There are really two issues here: Could you hurt him? and Would you hurt him?

Could you hurt him? It is possible, but given detailed instructions (for example, the ones in this book) and a reasonable amount of care, serious harm is exceedingly unlikely. Even a severe spanking won't kill him. But you may have a deep, hidden fear of the harm a Girl can do to a boy. Did your parents ever warn you against harming men? Try to bring these issues to the surface and deal with them before you set up your first scene.

Would you hurt him? That's another question entirely. Look inside yourself. If you do wish to hurt a man, please see a therapist and get rid of your rage before you try to act out your fantasies. I am not answerable for the consequences if you don't listen to this warning.

5.   *You don't believe that it's morally right for women to dominate men.* Your moral beliefs are between you and God. But if you are open to argument, please read the section of this chapter entitled "A Defense of Female Domination."

6.   *Your man (past or current) tried it and hated it. There's no point in trying again.* Yes, there is. Especially if the man who hated it is no longer your

partner. If your current man tried and disliked the experience, try talking with him about it. What was the problem? Was he uncomfortable with the intensity of his emotions? Did it evoke childhood feelings of helplessness or pain? Did he feel rushed into too deep a servitude? Did he feel uncomfortable using the safeword? Was there a specific act that bothered him? Would something else work better?

If discussions go nowhere (he won't talk or won't say more than that he hated it), maybe you do have to choose between acting out your fantasies or staying with your current partner. But more often, you'll find that he liked it, but it went on too long, or something you said reminded him of his mother (a sure passion-killer), or he simply felt silly wearing high heels and would have preferred to be tied up.

With time, a guilty Dominatrix can relax and enjoy enacting her most secret fantasies. You already possess the most important quality needed for a Mistress: the willingness to rule. Once you actually take charge, you (and the submissive males in your life) will have a wonderful time.

The Unwilling Dominatrix

The truly unwilling Dominatrix has no fantasies of controlling males. She may just be uninterested in playing games with the balance of power in her relationships; she herself may be submissive; or she may be revolted by the idea of hurting someone.

These three types – the Bored, the Submissive, and the Terrified – all deserve individual consideration.

- *The Bored.* If you are not interested in Female Domination, and several attempts have failed to arouse any spark of desire, try reading the rest of the book. You may simply never have found the right scenario. If nothing here appeals to you, it's probably safe to say that you are not and will never be a Mistress. No matter how fascinating others find the subject, you cannot be talked into Female Domination. Try another fantasy. You can be a sexually powerful, loving, strong woman without doing FemDomme.

- *The Submissive.* If you are a submissive yourself, you understand the joys of being Dominated, punished, and consoled. Consequently you may feel that the place over the knee is rightfully (and delightfully) yours. However, some of the best Dommes I know started out as submissives who widened their repertoire. Best of all, you don't have to give up the joys of submission in order to enjoy Dominance. As a switch, you automatically double your chances for a date at any play party, and you get the best of both worlds.

It's worth trying the Dominant role a few times to see if you enjoy it. You may prefer to have different partners for each role – one person to Domme you, another to sub to you – or you may enjoy switching with your primary partner.

If you yourself cannot do it, but the idea intrigues you, make up a wicked sister and step into her Dominant personality. Use your imagination to create a world in which you are the cruel Mistress and your partner is the infinitely punishable bad boy or sissy maid or whatever his specific fantasy is. If he is at all fair (and he should be), your mate will reciprocate with an evening of whatever kinky activities you crave.

Of course, you may find that you are a hard-wired submissive with no Dominant tendencies – but at least you've tried.

• *The Terrified.* If you are terrified or revolted at the thought of Female Domination, you may be facing one of two problems. (Maybe both.) Perhaps you believe that any Dominance play is sick, that it leads to the devaluation of Women or to real rape, mayhem, and murder, and that anyone who tries it is well on the way to becoming America's next serial killer. Or you may hold more tolerant opinions of Dominance play in general, but the idea of your taking part deeply distresses you. These two attitudes might be called the Political and the Personal.

Political Terror. Dominance play can be a difficult problem for a committed Feminist. (As a committed feminist myself, I should know.) I refuse to toss around sneering terms like "political correctness"; I respect your stand, though I disagree with it. But I would like to point out that power is ineradicable in people's lives, and that playing conscious games with it is far healthier than allowing it to remain potent and unexamined, causing problems behind the scenes. Aside from the usefulness of Women trying on the role of Tyrant, all consensual Dominance play teaches the shared, symbiotic use of power. Consent works both ways. Just as not all intercourse is rape, not all power games are evil manipulations.

Your objection could be more psychological: you may reject Dominance play because you are disgusted and frightened by the horrors of nonconsensual sadomasochism. You are right to fear the psychotic few. But the link between consensual fantasy and violent crime doesn't hold. People who engage in Dominance play or even in Dominance fantasy rarely commit sex crimes; most of them refuse even to hit their children, an act strongly endorsed by traditional culture. The two types of Dominance are totally different, not just in degree but in kind. I like to drive fast, but I'm no carjacker. I break the driving laws when I go over 65 mph, and so does a carjacker when he steals a Mercedes at gunpoint, but I don't think the two acts are comparable, or that driving too fast in my elderly station wagon will make me steal somebody's sports car. Or, to put it in other terms, somebody who enjoys a rare steak isn't necessarily a cannibal.

Doesn't consensual Dominance play lead to harder stuff? (Shades of Reefer Madness.) No. In fact, if Jung is to be trusted, people who are aware and accepting of their forbidden desires (the Shadow) are far less likely to have them erupt in a way that could devastate themselves and everyone around them. Anyone mentally healthy and aware enough to deal with Dominance fantasies in a consensual relationship is exceedingly unlikely to go on to nonconsensual activities.

There is a further logic problem to assuming that Dominance games lead to dreadful results. Don't fall into the trap of Krafft-Ebing, the Victorian psychologist who wrote the seminal work on sexual deviance, *Psychopathia Sexualis*. His case histories (which range from necrophiliacs to a man who had sex with a chicken) all gleefully note that, without exception, these perverts had been known to masturbate. Therefore masturbation caused their sick behavior. Unfortunately for the good doctor, almost everybody else masturbates, too, and few of us have been known to ravish domestic fowl, much less dig up graves. That's like saying that breathing air causes death, because all people who die have breathed air.

Personal Terror. If you are seriously distressed at the thought of Female Domination, you may be dealing with deeper issues than who gets tied up tonight. I will gently explore these issues, and then, as always, I will recommend that you discuss them with a competent therapist.

Perhaps that sounds comic, but I mean it seriously. If you are absolutely psychologically unable to take charge sexually, whether during intercourse or only in fantasy play, you have unnecessarily limited your range of expression. A therapist can help you find out why and help you free yourself from your fears and inhibitions.

The intense distress you feel at being asked to Dominate a man may even be cognitive dissonance: the clash of conflicting identities. Reared to be passive and accommodating to males, you are faced with an impossible situation: to accommodate the man you love, you must cease to be passive. This is a classic double bind; you cannot with any comfort or peace choose either alternative. Consequently, you are miserable. When you realize that he is miserable too, you may feel even worse. How can you make a fuss over such a small thing?

It is not a small thing, I assure you. The ordinary sex-stereotyping of our society is destructive enough; it makes Women who are strong or fat or smart or otherwise "different" feel like filthy, unlovable monsters, crimes against nature. (I will say that the Female Dominance culture is generally very accepting of such departures from the weak, thin, dumb blonde who is apparently the belle ideale of our culture.) Adding Female Dominance to the list may make you feel like a total freak.

Worse yet, you may have suffered additional experiences that sensitized you to the problem. For example, if you were reared with a violent father, as I was, ordering a man to do your bidding may be completely beyond you. You've learned to lie low, lest your abusive father destroy you. Any attempt to repress your feelings and force your way through the situation may result in serious psychological harm. Yes, at some point you must confront your terror and realize that your taking command, even in play, will not result in your instant destruction, but I beg that you will do so only in the care of a qualified counselor. This took me years of therapy, but the pain was well worth it, because I was able to reclaim my power not just in the sexual arena but in all the other areas of life where I had been hiding from my own strength.

Some Women reared in such dreadful family situations may not be passive, but may espouse egalitarianism with a zeal that makes Female Dominance – or any Dominance – psychologically impossible. If you are one of them, you will not serve, but you will not Rule, either. Power belongs to the cruel parent, and with a fierce pride you refuse to touch it. Your own carefully built self-image would shatter if you did, for you would be forced to see that you are like the monster who made your early life a misery.

Neither of these attitudes is especially healthy, though God knows they are understandable. Power in itself is not evil, and the playful exchange of power between consenting adults is a far cry from the thuggish brutality of an abusive adult terrorizing a helpless child. With professional help you can reclaim the strength in yourself that your mate sees and desires, and learn to exercise the Rule you were born for.

3

FINDING (OR CREATING)
A Submissive Male

"Attempt the end, and never stand to doubt; Nothing's so hard but that search will find it out." – Robert Herrick, "Seek and Find"

Inaugurating a lifetime of blissful Female Domination may be as simple as taking command one night in bed. Or it could be as time-consuming as placing a classified ad in the local alternative newspaper, screening your respondents, and choosing one for the honor of being your sissy maid. In ordinary circumstances, however, the process is laughably easy, once you've accepted your Dominant nature. (This chapter may be skipped by Mistresses who already possess a submissive male. You should proceed to Chapter 4, even if you've already begun to Rule him.)

Retraining Your Partner

The easiest way to find a male to Rule is to look in your own bed. As Dorothy so sagely observed, the best place to search for what you want is usually your own back yard. If you have Dominant stirrings, your partner has probably already responded to them, albeit unconsciously. In fact, he may have been attracted to you precisely because you are a Dominatrix.

In the days before I was conscious of my own Dominant desires, I was puzzled and amazed by the numbers of males who hinted to me that they sought to submit themselves completely to a Woman. I didn't even pick up all the hints at the time; many became clear only after I became a practicing Mistress. Yet I was giving off all the signals proper to Dominant Women: I was strong, sexual, confident, and perfectly willing to rub a male's nose in the dirt, at least during intellectual debates.

But even I, who was glad to demolish a male's intellectual pretensions with a single scorching phrase, needed to overcome a certain learned passiveness. Sexually and intellectually I was a tigress, but all too often during relationships I became a kitten, which was disappointing to males and damaging to me. Despite my natural sexual aggressiveness, taking that next step was a huge hurdle. Let me make it easier for you, dear Reader. I will tell you exactly how to teach your partner to accept Female Domination. (I presume you have already accepted it in yourself. If not, go back to Chapter 2.)

Easing Him Into It. You may wish to start him out gently, if you've been a passive partner so far. Start by taking command in bed. Don't just lie there and wait for him to touch you. Touch him. Pinch his nipples: most submissive males respond strongly to this, though some hate it (in which case it makes an excellent punishment). Stroke and knead his buttocks. Ask him to go down on you. Then, when you are ready for intercourse, get on top of him.

If he responds badly to all this energy on your part, you may have a problem. Possibly he is a Dom, in which case you need to talk. Or perhaps he is not a Dom, but just a jerk. Is he domineering and inflexible in other aspects of your life together? Is he intensely jealous and possessive of you? Does he take offense at your independence or your opinions? Is he touchy about his male pride? Maybe you should get a new man. Even if you're willing to keep Female Dominance no more than a private fantasy, consider dumping this guy. He could be dangerous. Even if he isn't, life is too short to waste on a macho jerk.

Most males, on the other hand, are thrilled when a Woman takes the sexual initiative. While sharing the afterglow, tell him how much you enjoyed taking charge. Ask him if he's ever fantasized about being dominated by a Lady. If he says yes or maybe, you are home free. Propose a fantasy session in the near future and skip to Chapters 5 and 6 to get full instructions on preparing the scenario.

Even if he doesn't admit to fantasizing about serving a harsh Mistress, he may be intrigued by the idea. Find out what his sexual fantasies are and try to blend them into a Dominance scenario.

For example, if he loves cunnilingus and can't get enough of it, suggest a scene in which worshipping at your Shrine is a reward for obeying you for an hour. Start him out on light obedience: hand-washing your panties, perhaps giving you a bath and then rubbing you all over with warmed lotion. If that idea arouses him (and if he's human, it should), act out the scene, remembering always to stay in command! You might slap his buttocks lightly for a fancied mishandling of your panties, but don't do a full-fledged spanking if he doesn't respond well.

Then allow him to offer you the oral servitude that is his reward. Once you've had as many orgasms as you please, allow him to come by masturbating with a pair of your panties, the silkier the better. Resist the temptation to push the scenario too far into heavy obedience or serious punishment. If he enjoys a pleasant first time, he will be hooked, and you will be well on your way to total control of a male.

If he isn't willing to try even such a simple scenario, you must not give up hope. Steer him toward catalogues, stores, and fiction that emphasize Female Rule. Only when he has made it clear that he isn't interested and never will be should you abandon hope.

The Deep End. If you've always been sexually aggressive with your partner, or if you've already tried out various fantasies together, your best bet might be to spring Female Rule on him. Plan the first scenario (using the instructions in Chapter 5 and 6) for a weekend when you both have time for lengthy sex play. This technique is more likely to fail when your male is under serious stress, so a weekend or vacation is the best time.

Then send him out for the newspaper and, when he returns, take over. You should already know him well enough to guess whether he would be more responsive to a Victorian Governess scolding him for disobedience and promising him a thorough caning, or a leather-clad Amazon threatening to tie him to the bed and use him sexually, or an imperious Queen demanding instant maid service. Tell him the safeword and then enjoy.

Afterward, discuss the details of the experience, your reactions, and his reactions, and make plans for another session. You're on your way to a zesty and satisfying life as a Female Tyrant.

Finding a Submissive Male

If you're currently between men, or you've decided to ditch your uncooperative partner, there are several ways to find a submissive. These suggestions also work well if you prefer not to be involved in a romantic relationship with your submissive, but simply want male maid service or submission.

Wanted: Sissy Maid for Dominant Vixen. One place to look for a partner in Dominance/submission games is the classified ads of your local alternative newspaper. Free weeklies such as the *City Paper* (published in Chicago, Philadelphia, Baltimore, and other cities) or unconventional newspapers such as the *Village Voice* offer reasonable ad rates; many have special sections for people looking for unusual sexual activities. Most even offer voice mail.

If you live in an area that doesn't support an alternative newspaper, you may still be able to use a classified ad. The specialized publications that cater to

Dominant Women and their partners offer classified ad sections with national distribution. Sometimes Women's ads are published for free in these publications, as long as you include a photograph of yourself. Many of the picture ads in these magazines are those of professional Mistresses, however. If you are an amateur Dominatrix seeking a continuing relationship, your ad may be misread. It's probably advisable to stick with the newsletters that feature word-only descriptions; they are aimed at a different audience.

You may choose to answer a man's ad, place your own, or do both. If you answer the ad of a submissive male, make sure your reply is not a supplication but a firm, even stern statement of your needs and desires. Do not permit him to try to boss you; many submissives test the prospective Mistress to see if she is really in charge. Stay in command!

Your own ad should be clear and authoritative, as befits a Dominatrix. Make it clear what you expect from the submissive: service only, a romantic relationship with full-time Dominance, or a romantic relationship with occasional sessions of discipline or maid service.

Many males ask to see a photograph with your reply, since they too often judge Women with their eyes only. You may choose to provide a standard photo or have a friend take specialized pictures of you in Mistress garb. (Use a Polaroid or digital camera, and black out your identifying features at first.) Or you may, quite rightly, refuse to provide any picture at all until you've established a rapport with the submissive. Remember, you are in charge. He is supplicating you for your favors. There are many more submissive males than Dominant Females, and they have to compete for our attention. (A great change from the meat-market singles-bar scene!)

If you do advertise or answer ads, follow some elementary safety tips when you respond to letters or messages. Correspond with the man or men for a while before you meet. Get to know more about the submissive than his fantasies. Is he someone you would be interested in dating, even if you weren't going to Dominate him? Does he sound sincere? Does he have any weird or dangerous ideas? What is his romantic history? His job history? Is he married?

When you do decide to set up a meeting, don't try to start off with a scene. Meet him for lunch in a public place to see if he is clean, attractive, tolerable. Tell a friend where you will be and with whom, and have a safe call set up, so she will call the cops unless you contact her at a specified time. Let him know he is on probation; you have other males applying for the position of sissy maid (or naughty schoolboy, or whatever), and you must interview all of them before you choose whom to honor with your Rule. Resist any pressure to go off with him right away; waiting sharpens desire. (Anyway, you are in charge, not him.) And get HIV tests before you even consider swapping any bodily fluids. Yes, I realize that you must wait six months for a clean test, but you don't want to die for a fantasy, do you?

Furthermore, sharing a satisfying Dominance scene absolutely requires knowledge of each other, knowledge not easily or quickly gained. You have to develop a rapport, a trust in one another. Two strangers trying to play out a fantasy together is just too pitiful and too unsatisfying for you, a Mistress, to endure. The one-night stand is for lesser Women who have not yet realized that they control their own sexual destiny, who fear (poor deluded Girls) that the male will vanish like smoke if he isn't instantly sated. As a Dominatrix, you know better than that.

Clubs and Social Groups. Another way to meet submissive males is through specialized social groups and clubs. If you wanted to meet a stamp collector, you would join the local philatelic society. If you want to meet a submissive male, join a group like PEP (People Exchanging Power), the Connecticut Leatherfolk, The Eulenspiegel Society, Black Rose, the Society of Janus, or your local group. They advertise in alternative papers and in the national newsletters for Dominant Women.

Although many groups accept only couples and single Women, usually the members know unattached submissive males who are clean, presentable, and disease-free. A personal recommendation is often the best way to meet a submissive. Furthermore, these groups can give you fresh ideas, emotional support, and an active social life. Even if you already possess a submissive, you might want to look them up.

Meeting Online. There are now so many websites, chat rooms, IRC channels, and forums devoted to various forms of BDSM that I cannot possibly list them all. My favorite is still and always the Adult Sexuality forum of CompuServe (GO HSX200), which offers a special section just for power exchange. The local style is definitely reflective and intellectual, rather than fantasy-based, but I know of more than a dozen marriages and five times that many serious, lasting relationships that started in HSX.

There are several potential pitfalls to meeting online. First, you may not know if your potential partner is telling the truth about his age, sex, marital status, looks, interests, level of experience, intentions, or anything else. If you do become interested in someone online, insist on taking plenty of time to get to know each other, talk on the phone as well as online, and ask for references from other people who have met him in 3D.

Second, online communication can be so intimate that it moves much faster than other forms of romance. It's easy to fall in love with someone who seems to echo your every thought, but that, in fact, is a clue that he's echoing, not necessarily telling the truth. Even if he is everything he claims to be, miscommunications and unspoken assumptions can wreck a romance. When all you see of one another is bare sentences, it's easy to fill in the background with what you want most, rather than dull old reality. Talk about everything that's important to you, not just your own developing passion. That's the way to keep things in perspective.

Third, he may be interested in hotchat or phone sex but not in a 3D relationship, or vice versa. Figure out what you want and make that clear up front. It's a waste of time and emotional energy to try cyberDommeing someone in hopes that you will someday meet, when he has no desire or expectation of taking the relationship past the screen. Likewise, if he wants a marriage to a Domme, and you want a stable of cybersubs to share hot fantasies, he's going to feel used and exploited if you don't make your intentions clear.

I've been burned myself in romance and friendship online by people who were insincere or exploitive. If he insists on keeping your relationship a secret, there is a reason. He may be sweet-talking you in one window while he woos the next victim in another.

I don't want to quench your enthusiasm for cyber, but it's a fast car on a very curvy road, and it needs a lot of skill and attention to control. Cyberscenes can be incredibly hot, and most of my best friends were met online. The information, support, friendship, and yes, romantic possibilities offered by online communication mean that everyone can have access to great kinky ideas – not just the lucky few who live in San Francisco or New York City.

4

MAINTAINING YOUR RELATIONSHIP:
Balancing Fantasy and Reality

"Marriage is a noble daring." – Dryden

The better your relationship before you try Female Dominance, the less likely you are to encounter problems after you first exercise your right to Rule. Nevertheless, any change in a relationship requires a period of adjustment, and beginning to play out sexual fantasies is no exception. This chapter will help you and your partner to adapt to the changes, avoid the pitfalls, and savor the benefits of a Feminine Regime.

Personality Changes and Potential Bad Reactions

Female Dominance may change you – and him – in unexpected ways. Although most of the changes will probably be positive, you could also encounter a problem or two.

It may seem that undue stress has been put on various psychological problems in the pages that follow; these warnings are not a sign that every couple who tries Female Domination is a pair of potential crazies, or that everyone who plays with power is secretly mad. However, Dominance play may remind people of various cultural or personal problems, and I would be irresponsible if I didn't address those issues. Most of you will experience minor problems, if any at all.

Your New Power. After you learn to demand, to command, and to control in your fantasy sessions, you may find yourself becoming more assertive in other situations as well. Especially if you were timid instead of confident, Girlish instead of Womanly, you may undergo a deep transformation. Such an increase in power is normal and natural. You have found a new forcefulness, a new will, in yourself, and you are eager to exercise it. More power to you; the world needs strong Women. However, your mate, your friends, and your colleagues may have a hard time dealing with your newly assertive ways. And you may even go a bit overboard at first, enjoying your new strength without considering how it affects others.

Where you once meekly let others interrupt you, you now speak up. Where you once offered ideas tentatively, as a question, you now offer decisive opinions backed up by shrewd arguments. You may hear comments about how much more energetic you seem, how much more confidence you have. You could attribute your new power to therapy or assertiveness training, if you like, or you could tell a few chosen friends about your adventures in the art of Female Dominance. Why not share the pleasure?

However, if you find yourself constantly interrupting others, scorning their ideas, or demanding service as a right from your colleagues, you may have gone too far. At home you may be Queen of all you survey, but at work and with friends, you should be a Woman of balance: strong, thoughtful, considerate, and firm. A Woman inhabits her own space fully but doesn't seek to conquer others' space, any more than she allows others to impose upon her. She competes – passionately – with her eyes on the goal, not with dirty tricks or cheap shots. And when she wins, she is gracious to those who haven't won.

If you have stepped a trifle beyond the line in your first transports of pleasure, do not blame yourself unduly. Time and awareness of others will help you grow accustomed to your Queendom. The giddy sensation of dawning power should settle into a calm self-confidence.

Bad Reactions – His. A man who has always longed to surrender his will to a Dominant Woman may find himself facing various ambivalent emotions the day after he has actually done so. Perhaps the session was disappointing. Or he disappointed himself by being able to endure less pain than he thought he could. Or he thoroughly enjoyed it but now feels less than manly. Or the session brought up frightening memories or emotions that he must grapple with or try desperately to repress.

- *The Disappointing Session.* This is probably the most common problem. Especially after years of fantasy, a real-life scenario can hardly live up to the fabulous intensity of the submissive's dreams. His fantasies may have involved deep humiliation, severe punishment, and slavish service, but he wanted all those things, done in that precise order and in that exact way. As abject and helpless as he seemed in those fantasies, they were carefully choreographed to suit his tastes.

Even the best-planned scenario may not measure up to fantasy. Few sessions are perfect, and some submissives may feel the whole scene is ruined by a single flaw.

Furthermore, there is an unavoidable distance between fantasy as it is dreamed and fantasy as it is enacted; they are never the same. In fantasies submissives bear intense pain bravely while totally under the command of an impossibly Dominant Female. The reality of a sore bottom and a slightly unsure Mistress – or even one who is confident but simply different than his dreams – may be a crashing disappointment to him. That gap between dream and reality can mar even a skilled Mistress's best efforts, especially the first time. This reaction is less and less common as you go on with Female Domination, as you understand each other's fantasies, grow accustomed to your new roles, and learn to relax and enjoy the mental dimension of the fantasy as much as the physical intensity.

Reactions to the imperfect session differ, depending on your submissive's temperament. He may become depressed, feeling he will never find the perfect Mistress. He may blame you for not living up to his standards, or he may simply feel that your Dominance style doesn't mesh well with his needs. If he accepts that the first time is never the best, that patience, practice, and communication can build a very satisfying fantasy-fulfillment, then he may be mildly disappointed but more excited that he has actually enjoyed what he so long desired.

The ideal way for both of you to respond to the disappointing session is to discuss what went wrong and why. The more you know about one another, the more openly you can discuss the action and the fantasy, what worked and what didn't, the better suited to one another you will become.

• *The Disappointed Submissive.* Sometimes the scene will go smoothly, but the submissive will be disappointed anyway – not in the session but in himself. He may have dreamed of taking heavy spankings and then found himself hurting and distinctly unaroused. Instead of gaining a sexual thrill from serving you, he found himself a little bored as he scrubbed out the toilet. Clearly he hasn't lived up to his own fantasies, or so he thinks.

The real problem here is that the two of you aren't engaging the fantasy intensely enough. Merely performing the actions appropriate to Dominatrix and slave aren't enough; you must spice them with fantasy. An inexperienced submissive cannot bear much pain, so you must make him believe that a very mild castigation is the most intense punishment possible. In the context of the fantasy, it is. See Chapter 5 for specific recommendations.

- *Post-Submission Anxiety.* You've gone through a very successful session, in which you kept the whip hand the whole time, forcing him into the submission he longed for, and giving him (and of course yourself) a spectacular release. Afterwards, he tells you that was the best, better a thousand times than any fantasy. So why is he anxious, hostile, apologetic, or depressed the next day?

  Post-submission anxiety generally occurs in a man who is secretly ashamed of his submissive tendencies. He may feel that he has lost or betrayed his manhood by submitting to you. He may feel sorry that he has "forced" you into doing something he finds shameful, selfish, or low. He may be feeling a sense of self-disgust that he ever indulged in such practices. He might even be disgusted with you for participating, or angry, or contemptuous.

  To some extent, you can soothe his anxieties by encouraging him to discuss them and listening calmly while he does. Offer reassurances appropriate to the situation and his feelings. Understand that mixed feelings are common about any sexual experience, much less one as heavily tabooed and emotionally charged as fantasy Dominance play.

  Many people involved in power-exchange play have ambivalent feelings about their fantasies and needs. Our society doesn't offer healthy models of that kind of sexuality. Instead it gives us the image of the Marquis de Sade or Jeffrey Dahmer for male dominance, and every crushed, bleeding battered wife ("see, they really enjoy it or they wouldn't stay") for female submission. And these are considered the natural gender roles!

  For those who defy the culture's prescribed gender roles, the situation is even bleaker. We have no image at all of Female Dominance, unless you count the desexualizing and vicious attacks on strong women in public life (they're always referred to as ballbusting bitches, and the remedy for their power is rape; their sexuality is supposed to be expressed entirely by castrating males). If a man wants to be submissive, he is a pussy-whipped Caspar Milquetoast and no real man at all. (Real men dominate Women, not submit to them.)

  During the heat of fantasy, it's easy to let the inner desire drown the voices of the censorious. But the next day, the cultural models may come back to haunt you – or him. If your submissive male feels ambivalent on the morning after, it's only natural. However, if he tries to reassert his maleness by (literally or metaphorically) pushing you around, stop him immediately. You cannot get into that kind of game. If necessary, stop playing out your fantasies while you work out the problem. You may want to see a couples counselor or seek individual therapy to help you deal with the anxieties.

- *Flashbacks and Bad Memories.* If anxieties persist, or serious depression results from fantasy play, your submissive may be reliving certain painful memories. Many people who are involved in power exchange play had healthy, normal childhoods but became fascinated with the idea of Dominance and submission. Others had the kind of nightmare experiences usually associated with daytime talk-show guests. I am not prepared to discuss whether all Dominance/submission play is a displacement activity or a Freudian taboo-turned-ritual or a working-out of cultural roles or even a product of reincarnation; we just don't know enough to theorize effectively, and anyway I am concerned with practice here, not origins. All I can say is that some people who have Dominance/submission fantasies also have other serious power issues, and that acting out the fantasies can awaken those issues.

    What do you do if he starts having nightmares, or becomes seriously depressed, or starts having flashbacks? Stop playing and see a competent therapist. Immediately!

    Serious Warning Signs. If he (or you) starts to show any of the signs of serious emotional disturbance, get help and get it fast. If one of you becomes violent, depressed, or inappropriately filled with rage; can't stop crying or can't get up to do anything at all; starts thinking or talking of suicide, get help now. (Although very, very few players ever have such bad reactions, you have to know what to watch for, just in case.)

Bad Reactions – Yours. Your reactions may be similar to his. You could be disappointed in the scene or in yourself, or feel anxious over defying the cultural norm. You too could suffer from flashbacks or other intense emotional reactions.

- *The Disappointing Scene and the Disappointed Mistress.* These two problems go together, because your identity as a good Mistress is presumably bound up in how well the scene goes. If it doesn't work out perfectly, you may feel totally responsible. After all, you are in charge. You planned it, you were the Dominant one, and if you fumbled, or your submissive seemed disappointed, you may feel like a failure.

    If you do, reread the section on his disappointment. Few first (or second, third, twentieth) scenes go perfectly smoothly. Remember losing your virginity? That too was probably awkward, painful, embarrassing, or flawed, but that (I hope) didn't stop you from trying again. A fulfilled sexuality, despite MTV and the advertising industry, isn't readily purchased whole, like (or in) a tube of toothpaste. You have to work at it. (Pleasant work, but it does take effort, intimacy, and commitment.) So it isn't necessarily your fault, and you shouldn't give up just because you forgot how to fasten his bonds or neglected to give him something he wanted. (And if he never told you he wanted it, that's his fault, not yours.) Keep discussing fantasies, find out what worked and what didn't, and go on.

What about your own satisfaction? This is, after all, Female Dominance, and if you aren't getting what you want from a scene, you need to re-evaluate your technique. It helps at first to have an idea of what you do want from any scene: a sense of freedom and power, or lots of stroking and orgasms, or a perfect pedicure. I've done plenty of scenes where I didn't get any orgasms, but I don't always want them. Sometimes I want Domme-gasms – that wonderful rush of power from being able to express the deepest parts of myself with a willing submissive.

- *Post-Dominance Anxiety.* Whatever your personal situation, you were raised in a culture that demands that Girls be nice. Dominance isn't nice. Fun, yes. Fulfilling, absolutely. But not nice. The next day, you may feel apologetic for hurting him or bossing him around. Worse, you may feel that you've violated who you are. (You may want to reread Chapter 2.) The glimpse of power you had may be frightening; you could be watching a whole new self coming to birth.

   Talk about it. Write a journal about it. Don't just sit and stew, worrying that you're becoming a monster. In all likelihood, you aren't. But if you have no one to talk to – your submissive may not want to discuss it, your friends would be horrified – find a support group. You are rebelling against all sorts of cultural imperatives by becoming a Dominatrix, and you need the support and help of your Sisters.

   Many cities have a chapter of PEP (People Exchanging Power) or local support groups (Black Rose in Washington, DC, the Society of Janus in San Francisco, and the Eulenspiegel Society in New York, for example). You may need to travel to find playgroups and support groups; it's not uncommon for people to drive four or five hours to attend a gathering. I live in an intensely rural area, but I only have to drive for two hours north or south to find support.

   Look for other Mistresses' ads in the local free weekly (professionals may not be helpful) or put an ad in yourself, suggesting that you create a

Dommes' group for discussion, support, friendship, and the exchange of evil ideas.

Online forums can give even the most isolated Mistress a chance to make friends with Dommes from around the world, as well as to meet GuyDoms (who can be incredibly helpful friends) and subs of both conventional genders. GuyDoms also have to overcome early training ("Don't hit girls!") and can become solid buddies, even if they do turn green and cross their legs when you talk about CBT. Subs of whatever gender and orientation can help convince you that yes, they really do like this! That can be a big help if your sub is not especially communicative.

I've known at least one Domme whose experiences with her first sub were so difficult that she thought of giving up. However, when she sought and found support from others, she discovered that there was nothing wrong with her instincts or actions; she was just sadly mismatched with her submissive. Dommes tend to feel responsible for everything, and she had blamed herself.

Or, if you feel you'd like to explore some of these issues in depth, talk to a sympathetic therapist.

- *Flashbacks and Bad Memories.* If your anxieties persist, or serious depression results from fantasy play, you may be reliving certain painful memories. Whatever the facts of your childhood, you may have come to associate wielding power with a devastating indifference toward or even active hatred of the less-powerful person. In your childhood, that was almost certainly you. To find yourself suddenly in the position of the tormentor can cause an intolerable psychological shift.

  If you feel this way, get help now. Don't just vow to quit Female Dominance; you cannot avoid the issue of power. At some point you must face it, and better sooner than later.

  Serious Warning Signs. If you starts to show any of the signs of serious emotional disturbance, get help and get it fast. If you become violent, depressed, or inappropriately filled with rage; can't stop crying or can't get up to do anything at all; start thinking or talking of suicide, get help now. (Although very, very few players ever have such bad reactions, you have to know what to watch for, just in case.)

- *A Final Note.* Despite all the warnings and concerns, I assure you that most people who play Dominance games are actually happier with each other than couples who cannot share their deepest needs and desires, whatever they may be. Nevertheless, as a responsible Mistress and author, I feel I should let you know about some possible items of concern. Even if one or several of these problems arise between you, you can overcome them if your relationship is strong. After a brief period of adjustment, you should both become comfortable in the new roles, whether you play occasionally or all the time.

Changes In Your Relationship

Just as acting out your fantasies may have brought up personal issues of power and Dominance, it may do so with issues between the two of you. The individual changes are bound to affect you as a couple. Honest discussion of the issues and your feelings can help keep your relationship strong; indeed, the intimacy and trust created between you, as well as your more active role in the relationship, are bound to make the commitment stronger and deeper than ever before. What follows are a list of suggestions for dealing with Dominance issues and a list of the benefits Female Dominance can bring to your relationship.

Dealing with Dominance Issues: Some Suggestions

• *Keep Dominance in Its Place.* Female Dominance is a wonderful game, but it has its limits. You and your mate must decide what they are. Some couples use it as an occasional spice a few times a year. Others prefer to play monthly or weekly, while maintaining a vanilla sexual life or exploring other fantasies (even including male dominance). Many couples enjoy full-time Female Dominance, but they are beyond the scope of this book. The two of you should decide early on approximately how often you want to have scenes and what your signal should be to communicate that desire.

  You must keep Dominance games in their place in another way: never use a discipline session to work out a problem in your relationship or to take out your anger on your submissive. If you have a conflict in the relationship, work it out by talking about it. Don't get it mixed up with sexual games, unless you've already negotiated the right to punish.

• *Stay Safe, Sane, and Consensual.* The watchword for Dominance/submission play has always been that it is safe, sane, and consensual. Keep to those principles. Don't take stupid risks or do things you know are dangerous. Keep other emotional problems out of the dungeon. And never play unless both participants are willing. Either of you has the right to say no to Dominance play, just as you may say no to any other sexual contact. And never bring in unwilling or unwitting partners or witnesses to your games. That's a species of psychological rape.

• *Honor Your Commitment.* Always treat one another with respect. Don't mock your partner's fantasies the day after a session, or tell your best friend about your activities without your mate's consent. Yes, I've said you should find people you can share your experiences with, but you must honor the privacy of what you do together. Talk to your mate before you talk to others.

- *Talk.* Communication is the key to a good relationship, and you should always be able to discuss everything together, from the awkward feelings occasionally arising from a scene to daring new fantasies. The more intimate you become, the better your sessions will be, and vice versa. In the exhausted, satisfied moments after you've achieved release and ended a scene, you may tap into deep emotions you've never shared with anyone else. You can share them now, with your partner.

- *Relax.* Despite all the warnings, Female Dominance is a game, and a wonderful one. Relax and enjoy it. Don't expect it to be perfect. Just enjoy the pleasures of command, of stepping beyond your ordinary boundaries and becoming another person. Your submissive should relax, too. The scene may not be exactly what he dreamed of, but then, what he wanted was to lose control, not to keep it. He should let go and feel the intoxicating freedom of utter submission.

The Benefits of Female Domination

- *A Clean House.* A recent survey indicated that 61% of Women would rather see a man do housework than dance naked. They would also rather be married to a Danny DeVito lookalike who did the dishes than a Robert Redford lookalike who didn't. You can use his fantasies of submitting to a Female Tyrant not only for mutual sexual satisfaction, but also to keep the house looking spotless. If you loathe housework and he gets an erotic thrill from running the vacuum, I'd say you have an ideal partnership.

- *A More Equal Relationship.* Partly because he's doing some or all of the housework, your relationship will become more equal when you begin to practice Feminine Rule. Your new assertiveness will carry over into other parts of the relationship, and his experiences of being out of control of his own destiny should help him understand just how hard a Woman's life can be.

- *More Intense Sex.* Even an occasional dose of fantasy can serve to keep your sexual flame burning bright. As a careful, loving Mistress, you'll get to know all the most sensitive spots on your lover's body, a knowledge you can turn to good use when you're having more conventional sex. Furthermore, you'll learn to ask for what you want in bed. Sex is always better between two active, involved partners. Perhaps most important, the two of you will keep your imaginations active and alive; boredom kills sexual desire faster than anything else except sheer physical exhaustion.

- *Deeper Trust.* Rarer than good sex is trust. And once you've shared your innermost fantasies with someone who helps you act them out, who doesn't mock or recoil or injure you, you know you have established trust. The shared vulnerability of acting out fantasies can create a wonderful new intimacy. Nothing can strengthen a relationship like trust.

Part Two

THE MISTRESS IN ACTION

5

ESTABLISHING YOUR AUTHORITY:
Ways to Make Him Obey

*"That not impossible she/Who shall command my heart and me." –
Richard Crashaw, "Wishes to His Supposed Mistress"*

Even before you plan and enact the first session, you must understand
whence derives the authority of a Mistress. Establishing that authority is the first
thing a Mistress must do; the best-scripted session will fail if the submissive
cannot believe in and surrender to the Dominion of his Lady.

What follows is a discussion of half a dozen ways to establish and enforce
your authority, even while you are receiving the shattering pleasure of orgasm.
Some are more effective than others, but when all are used judiciously, in their
proper proportion, they will produce a contented submissive and a fulfilled
Dominatrix.

Some of these ideas may seem far-fetched. Nevertheless, ordinary life, with
all its worries, fears, and stresses, has a death grip on most of us. We need all the
help we can get to move into the realm of fantasy. Deliberately choosing to suffer
pain and suspense as a path to a happy conclusion can exorcise the demons of doubt,
fear, tension, and misery that most of us struggle with every day. Changing our
names, our clothes, our surroundings, our behavior, can help us free the repressed
inner self. The suggestions below offer ways to break the stranglehold of reality
and move into the glorious, softly lighted, ritualistic domain of our hidden selves.

The Script

Because Chapter 6 is devoted to the art of planning, structuring, and
enacting an effective discipline scenario, I will not say much about it here, except

to remind you that good scripting is the first essential. A satisfying script will provide both Mistress and slave with a thoroughly meaningful experience. Remember that it's the story that takes you and your submissive out of your everyday selves, invests you with almost magical powers, and ultimately provides release.

Every technique I discuss in this chapter is a way to emphasize the story and make it more vivid, intense, and believable. A hastily sketched, carelessly plotted fantasy is as boring as most television. If TV effectively relaxed you and your partner, you wouldn't be reading this book. You need a deeper, more individual ritual than you find in mass media. And books, wonderful as they are, cannot be shared in the same way. Besides, sometimes you need to act. Thus the script, the fantasy, and your compelling role as Mistress.

Furthermore, a good script will help you, the Mistress, remember who you are: the Woman in charge. It also provides us with the useful theatrical metaphor, which so accurately describes all phases of the Dominance/submission relationship that it might not be a metaphor at all, but the literal truth.

Pain and Suspense. When most people think of Female Dominance, they think of pain, and that is a great pity. Although sensation play has its place in a scene, it is not necessarily the most important element. Suspense, the linchpin of good drama, is far more important, although it cannot stand alone. Because pain and suspense work together so closely, I have decided to deal with them as twin aspects of a single topic.

To make any scene work, you must build suspense in your subject. Pain alone, even humiliation alone, will not produce the tension and then the release he needs. Relying on physical pain to produce effective subordination (a crude technique at best) ultimately fails, because you have not made the pain meaningful.

Havelock Ellis, one of the earliest experts in sexual psychology, wrote that suspense, not suffering, is what the submissive truly desires. For example, a strange Woman walking up to him and slapping him would scarcely make him feel aroused. The incident might later provide a basis for fantasies, in which the submissive would construct a story to explain the pain, thereby adding suspense and significance. In short, it is the plot – the enacted drama – not the punishment that gives the submissive release.

Controlling a male's body does not suffice to control his mind. Otherwise, he would spend every minute of his work day thinking of work, every minute at the dinner table thinking of food, and so on. You should know that even when he is bound to a backboard or forced into ladies' clothing, you must supply him with fantasies (the script) or his mind will wander. In such situations, of course, his mind is likely to wander toward fantasy anyway, but they are his fantasies, which he chooses and controls, and will not be as effective for him and satisfying for you as the fantasies and ideas you introduce. Even a heavily symbolic punishment, such as spanking, can be felt as meaningless pain unless accompanied by a compelling fantasy – and again, yours, if well-chosen and enticingly presented, will work better than his own.

No, the only way to control even the most lamb-like submissive is to control his thoughts. Suspense is one of your most efficacious tools to command your submissive's wandering attention. Anyone can inflict pain, but few people can make it erotic and fulfilling. If raw pain were really what he craved, he could get into bar fights and be equally happy or even happier, or drive his car into a bridge and suffer for months in a body cast. Neither of these dreadful ideas (which I sincerely beg you will not consider, even for a moment) is in the least erotic.

Therefore, if you give him a smaller dose of pain, but a greater measure of suspense, he will obey you more readily and respect you more thoroughly, and you both will be more fulfilled. Using suspense effectively is the first mark of a top-notch Disciplinarienne, even one who enacts the role of Amazon or Governess.

Mystery and Anticipation. Now that suspense has been demonstrated to be vital to the successful establishment of your authority, you may be asking precisely how you can use suspense, or even how to create it in the first place.

The two elements of suspense are mystery and anticipation. Although they would seem to be mutually exclusive, they actually work well together in the hands of a skilled Mistress.

Mystery is based on surprise; the submissive wonders what will happen next, and alternately hopes and fears ("maybe Mistress won't punish me... but she always does").

Anticipation is based on recognition; the submissive knows exactly what will happen next, and endures the same vacillation ("maybe it won't hurt so much this time... but last time it did").

The pleasure of the changing seasons is exactly the same mingling of mystery and anticipation. Each spring is the same, but each is different. We enjoy both recognition and surprise when the daffodils bloom every year. To make the same three or four fantasies constantly interesting, you must vary them slightly: enough to be fresh and exciting, not enough to distort their message. If you fall into a routine with your fantasy script, always scolding him for the same crime and punishing him in the same way, your submissive will sense no mystery and feel no anticipation, and will soon grow restless and dissatisfied.

Foster the sense of mystery by doing things slightly differently each time. Try out new sensations and new variations on the fantasy. (I provide suggestions for these later in the book.) If he is never quite sure what will happen next, whatever you do will have extra power. Add to the mystery by letting him think you plan one particular chastisement and then at the last minute altering it slightly in duration, instrument, audience, or style. You can also make mysterious promises or allow him glimpses of a new costume or implement, and then watch the suspense work in him.

Encourage anticipation by telling him precisely what you plan to do, and then making him wait for you to do it. Gauging a vassal's readiness to be punished is a delicate matter. You must let him suffer anticipation long enough to extract all the pain from the waiting but no so long as to leave him feeling bored and neglected.

Careful attention to maintaining proper suspense means that you will need to inflict less physical pain. By involving his mind, you create a better scene and earn him a deeper catharsis.

Inflicting Punishment: Ending the Suspense. The threat of punishment and the suspense of awaiting punishment are all very well. But at some point, you will have to actually punish your submissive. When you do so, your submissive should feel that the suspense of waiting has been so dreadful that he could not have borne it for one more second, while still facing the actual chastisement with fear and trembling. (The techniques of punishment are discussed in Chapters 7 and 8, with notes in each fantasy chapter for the best use of these methods.) Nevertheless, the Dominance you show is far more important than the pain you inflict.

Almost all punishment a Mistress inflicts is done with the (implied) consent of the submissive. To be honest, few Disciplinariennes are muscular enough to enforce their commands on an unwilling submissive male, at least not without an unbecoming struggle. Most of us rely on moral authority and the power of Dominance, coupled with occasional bouts of severity.

Thus, establishing your authority over the male is essential. You must make him acknowledge your command and dread crossing you in any way. Only then will your chastisements be significant. Although physically he could fight you off and escape the punishment, that choice must be unthinkable to him. He must be willing to lie over your lap to be spanked, knowing he could escape but refusing to do so, because escaping would ultimately be more painful than any whipping could possibly be. The threat of worse whippings is not enough to produce that state of mind. Only psychological Dominance can do so.

The Language of Power

From punishment to language seems a strange and unexpected leap, yet one of the Mistress's strongest tools is language. In a later section, we will consider the use of the voice itself in establishing your command, but now we are looking at the power of mere vocabulary.

The Dominance Name. The proper choice of words can both express and sustain your power in the relationship. The simplest demonstration of this great truth is how your submissive addresses you during a session. I doubt that he calls you Sugar, Toots, or the Old Ball-and-Chain. Instead he calls you by your Dominance name: Ma'am, Mistress, or perhaps Mistress Lorelei. Such formality is conducive to discipline and a proper atmosphere of submission. Some Nursemaids and Governesses like to be addressed as Miss or Mrs. Jones, using their own last name or one they have chosen for its disciplinary connotations. (Miss Birch is very popular; so is Miss Marwood, for the great fictional Governess.) Others prefer to be called Mama or Auntie while they are correcting their charges.

The effect of the change of your name is immense. When your submissive calls you by your Dominance name, he must acknowledge your authority and your power. Furthermore, he realizes that he is not now dealing with his wife or girlfriend, but with a Female Tyrant whom he must obey or suffer the consequences. The change of identities establishes your influence during scenes and helps you maintain a healthy relationship the rest of the time.

Not only should you select a Dominance name and strictly enforce its use, you must also choose a new name to bestow on your submissive. Brook no arguments from him about what names he likes or wants. You must provide his new identity in order to control him whenever you invoke it. Addressing him by his submission name is an unmistakable signal that the Dominance session is about to begin. After some practice, he will slip into obedience and passivity as soon as you call him by his submission name, just as you will take command whenever you hear your Dominance name.

What names are effective choices for a submission name? Males who dream of being sissy maids respond to such frilly Feminine names as Cindy, Yvette, or Bitsy. Males who desire a Governess or Nursemaid respond best to childhood nicknames, especially diminutives (Bobby, Freddy, Ricky) or during discipline to his full name: "Robert Edward Jones, bend over!"

Other Dominance Names. In the world of childhood, every object is known and named. You must strive to recreate this atmosphere in your fantasy sessions. Thus you should give Dominance names to your favorite discipline implements and techniques as well as to your various body parts.

The names should emphasize female power and harmonize with the submissive's fantasies. A certain playfulness in naming adds a special fillip to the names. A much-feared paddle might become Mistress Pattycake. A naughty submissive in need of bondage could be told that he must spend some time with Mistress Bonnie. The invitation to wear some pretty jewelry could refer to the attachment of nipple clamps.

Genitalia should also be named, partly because there are few really pleasant or attractive words in English for them, partly in order to heighten the atmosphere of a secret world. Choose a powerful and sexy name for your Femaleness. Mistress Gloria or Mistress Victoria are good names, because they are simultaneously suggestive of the wonders within and easy to slip into apparently innocent conversations. Tell a submissive, "You need to spend some time with Vicky, dear," and he is instantly aware that you are demanding a long session of cunnilingus. And that's the sort of message you could leave with a secretary without embarrassment to either her or you.

It is also your duty to rename his genitalia. The name should emphasize his juvenile and inferior status without being so mocking as to render him impotent. A slightly childish name for his penis and two alliterative names for his testicles will equip you to tease and torment him to your heart's content.

Appropriate Set and Props

Setting also contributes a great deal to the effectiveness of the scene. If you have space enough to set aside a room for play, you may decorate it as fantasy dictates: as a dungeon, a schoolroom, or a frilly bedroom. Most of us have limited space, but an ordinary room may be decorated with subtle hints of domestic discipline: with a four-poster bed, wooden hairbrushes, and attractive ribbon-tied arrangements of birch branches. If your submissive desires to be disciplined by a stern schoolmarm, buy an antique school desk to bend him over, and hang a framed blackboard above the scene for his punishment writings or to display your written judgment of his naughtiness.

You may also wish to enhance the mood with carefully chosen lighting, music, incense, or other sense stimulators. However, do choose carefully. The incense and candles natural to an Amazon or Goddess fantasy are totally out of place in a schoolroom or nursery setting. Nor would a sissy maid fit naturally into a black-painted dungeon.

Props, of course, would include all the delightful implements of correction, humiliation, and restraint, from a leather strap to audiotapes of punishment sessions to the very Victorian backboard, but these implements vary depending on fantasy, and are discussed under their individual fantasy headings.

But why should you, the Mistress, trouble to create a particular atmosphere at all, much less decide whether your male slave would prefer a warm and cozy nursery or a stern prison cell? Because the point of fantasy is escape, and the emotional release is amplified by taking place in a congenial setting. Your fantasies will be far more effective if they are enacted in their proper environment.

Costumes

Extreme care must be taken in the selection of appropriate costumes for Dominatrix and submissive, for this aspect of the fantasy is almost as crucial to a satisfying session as a properly chosen method of castigation, especially at first.

It's a vile generalization to assert that men are sexually aroused by what they see, but it's usually true. Most guysubs have spent years visualizing exactly how the Mistress of their dreams will dress. If you want a direct grip on his libido, your clothing and makeup can provide it. Moreover, certain clothes can become a subtle or not-so-subtle signal that it's time to play. Whether it's that special shade of burgundy lipstick or a particular pair of shoes, your Mistress garb can arouse you both.

Depending on your comfort and desire and on the chosen fantasy, you may appear in a severe business suit, in a slip and stockings, or in thigh-high leather boots and matching corset, though in my experience it's hard to swing a flogger when you're confined that way.

A simple black T-shirt and matching jeans can be as effective a costume as all the leather-and-steel regalia in the world. You need to decide how much of your submissive's visual sense you want to please, how much you want to tease. Also, frankly, how much do you enjoy dressing up? If you love it, you can choose elaborate outfits by fantasy. Or you can relax and say the hell with it. You're the Domme, remember.

Likewise, the submissive could be wearing anything from nothing at all to diapers. The fantasy itself usually dictates which types of clothing should be worn.

That some change of clothing is necessary is mandated by the principles we have been using all along. The better the scene-setting, the better the fantasy.

Every day you judge people by their clothing, so instantaneously that you may not be aware that you are classifying the people you pass as students, homeless, wealthy, artistic, working-class, or computer nerds. You may not always be accurate, but you do read the clothing messages others offer.

Still doubtful? Consider the effect of uniforms. When a man in a white coat wearing a stethoscope tells you to undress, you probably do. In the same office, with the same man dressed as a policeman, making the same request, you would demand his strip-search warrant and then comply. If a man in a hard hat told you to do so, you would refuse unless he were your lover. You don't usually ask the man in white to prove he is the doctor whose diplomas hang on the wall. Instead, the power of the uniform convinces you.

You can take advantage of this effect by dressing in a way that spells power to your submissive, and for every male that costume is different. Find out his fantasies, look at the pictures of Dommes that he collects, and you can deduce his internal image of Female authority. By dressing to invoke that image, you can exert greater power over him with less effort.

Costume also has an influence, not only on how others see us, but on how we see ourselves. Your Domination garb should make you feel proud, stern, magnificent. Whether you select black leather embellished with metal studs or a Lady's riding habit circa 1890, the costume should mean power to you as well.

Likewise, when you dress a male in Women's clothing, he feels helpless, excited, and ashamed, all at once. Dressing him as a baby, a schoolboy, or a prisoner will similarly alter the way he acts. There is also the very practical consequence that a half-naked male or one dressed in a French maid's uniform cannot very well escape from your control. He would be too ashamed if someone else saw him dressed as his secret fantasy.

And that fantasy is the real key. If a vassal is dressed properly, his hidden self is both revealed and defined by his clothing. Costumes remove inhibitions because they change identity. Even a doctor might hesitate to tell you to undress without her stethoscope and white coat.

Persuasive Acting

Perhaps acting is the wrong word here. But, as I am using a theatrical metaphor throughout the book, I may as well continue. When I speak of acting, I am not in any way assuming that you are insincere in your Dominance. I intend acting to signify the techniques an actress uses to convey a character: voice, gesture, and carriage. A great script if poorly performed may be a bore. Thus your Dominance cannot be complete unless everything you say and do expresses it: not just your words but also your voice; not just your actions but your very body language. You have to live the part.

Tone of Voice. Many Women speak apologetically, in soft, scared little voices more suited to Girls than grown Women. Learn to speak firmly, sometimes even harshly, to your submissive. If you have problems, practice using a tape recorder. You'll find it extraordinarily liberating to use your voice to its fullest potential, to let all your forbidden emotions be revealed in your voice.

Try varying your tone of voice. Does he respond more to a sweet, mocking tone or to an abrupt, commanding tone? In all cases, you should speak with assurance and authority. You will convince both him and yourself that you are in charge.

Gesture and Carriage. Commonly known as body language, gesture and carriage include such nonverbal communications as eye contact, facial expression, and body stance. The way you walk, sit, stand, smile, and hold your chin both express and determine whether you are Dominant or submissive in any situation. The Dominant person maintains eye contact, while the submissive drops his gaze. The Mistress moves strongly, with free strides and broad gestures, while the submissive limits the amount of space he takes up. The Dominatrix smiles rarely, the slave often. The Dominant Woman is free to look where she pleases, while the male cringes and looks away. The Mistress holds up her head, the submissive hangs his. By moving with confidence, you can Rule him without a word.

Preparing for the Part

Before a discipline session, you might wish to spend some time getting yourself into the role of Dominatrix. Review your script, check your implements, and practice your Mistress voice and carriage. Until you can snap into your Dominant state instantaneously, with no thought, a little rehearsal is conducive to a smooth-running and successful fantasy.

When you have become a skilled Mistress, you may not need such extensive preparation. But it is always wise to remember that the Mistress cannot take her authority for granted. You must earn it with the force and vividness of your fantasies, the effectiveness of your disciplinary methods, and the compelling power of your personality.

Pleasure

One of the best ways to establish and maintain your authority is by enjoying Domination. When your submissive sees the pleasure he can give you, he feels happy and grateful and needed; he wants to give you more. Certainly there are moments when pleasure is inappropriate; some submissives never want to see the Mistress smile. But the vast majority want you to be having a good time, especially when you are punishing or consoling them. Otherwise he may feel that you don't like Female Domination and are doing it unwillingly, and therefore that he is secretly directing the action.

Your showing pleasure may entail as little as smiling sternly when you brandish the birch or as much as multiple orgasms. Show delight in all the various scenes of the fantasy – enjoying his costume, smiling when you threaten to punish him, and so forth. After all, a happy Mistress makes a happy slave.

Showing delight, of course, is predicated on your feeling delight. If you're not having a good time, adjust your scene until you are.

6

ASSERTING YOUR DOMINANCE:
Planning, Structuring, and Enacting Your First Session

"Charisma knows only inner determination and inner restraint.... The charismatic leader gains and maintains authority solely by proving [her] strength in life." – Max Weber, "Economy and Society"

Satisfying scenes don't just happen, any more than the plays of Shakespeare just happened. Great fantasies, like great drama, must be planned, considered, and choreographed before the performance. Once you know the script by heart and understand the dynamics of the drama, you may improvise as much as you like. At first, however, it's best to plan – if only so you have all the toys you want ready to hand, instead of having to rummage through a toybag looking for a blindfold.

Naturally, I am in no way suggesting that you must write out every line you plan to speak to your submissive. A too-rigid style of play is as bad as one that is too loose. I am reminding you to put some effort into the planning of your sessions, especially the first one. Proper self-discipline in the Mistress shows in a thoroughly and happily disciplined slave. When you take the trouble to understand the needs of your submissive, you are doing him the kindest possible favor. For example, if he needs humiliation and gets mere punishment, he may rebel. No Mistress desires an insolent submissive; it reflects so badly upon her governance of him.

Moreover, by planning a script, you are creating a satisfying scene for yourself – a scene you will find erotic, empowering, joyful, or whatever else you desire. Sometimes it's easy for us to be so focused on the sub's needs, limits, landmines, fears, experience, and desires that we forget our own. Yes, you have to take all those factors into account. But your own pleasure matters too. A good script can help you remember that.

Your fantasy script provides the context that determines the significance of what you do. One of the major differences between Domestic Discipline and Leather is the overt fantasy roleplaying of the Domestic Discipline style. Yet even the Leather community has its mythos, its sense of itself as a group apart, its costumes and props, its private meanings for words like "sadist" and "slut." In a very real emotional sense, a LeatherDomme may well own her submissive, but no court in the land would uphold that ownership. It is simultaneously absolutely true and absolutely untrue – like all myths. And like all myths, this one is designed to create and express a world.

Determine His Needs

Your first step in planning an effective discipline session is to determine your submissive's needs. He may not, in fact, need actual discipline (in the sense of physical punishment) as much as he needs humiliation, subjection, servitude, or feminization.

Find out what he needs by talking to him. Command him to tell you his three favorite fantasies, and take careful note of any recurring elements. If in each fantasy he is forced to wear ladies' ruffled panties, you know that lingerie (and probably Feminization or humiliation or both) is an essential part of his needs.

You might choose to give him a foretaste of your Regime by forcing him into the confession of his fantasies. Nipple-pinching, an excellent persuader, will leave him panting for a real dose of your Reign. (Do not permit him to have an orgasm yet, no matter how much he begs for one. You must control the timing and frequency of his orgasms from now on. Giving in to him only encourages whining, an unattractive trait.) Analyze his fantasies by comparing them to the five archetypal Female Dominance scenarios adduced in Chapter 9. Then you will be able to proceed with self-assurance as well as open curiosity.

If this first scene is meant to be a surprise, get access to his collection of books and magazines on the subject of Ladies' Rule. If he has a secret stock of implements, better yet. You should be able to determine from his reading matter and accessories just what sort of fantasy he cherishes. Canes, hairbrushes, and spanking magazines all point to the Governess fantasy, while a hidden store of diapers, rattles, and baby bottles infallibly indicates a taste for the Nursemaid's tender ministrations.

If, after perusal of his favorite reading matter, you still cannot determine his tastes, he may be an eclectic submissive. In which case, choose your favorite fantasy from among the five archetypes, and plan your strategy accordingly. You can always take a few moments during that first session to torment him into confessing his secret desires. By eliciting and fulfilling them at once, you save energy and provide a little entertainment. I told you it was fun to be a Mistress, didn't I?

What Do Women Want?

Freud asked this famous question, which in a somewhat twisted way answers itself. Women want respect – which in this case, means not being lumped together as an alien species incapable of being understood.

What you want in scene may be anything from a chance to try out your new bondage skills to fourteen orgasms in a row. You may just want the thrill of command, sometimes known as a Domme-gasm. Figure out what you want and plan to get it.

Plan a Pleasing Scenario

The essential principle of the pleasing scenario is drama. The scene should be crafted like a well-made play. You must provide an effective plot and script; appropriate set, props, and costumes; and persuasive acting.

Plot and Script. The details of your script should be based on your submissive's known needs and fantasies – and of course your own. However, almost all Female Dominance fantasies follow more or less the same pattern. This ritual is the private drama that provides catharsis for your submissive. It goes like this: You establish your authority; he transgresses; you punish him; you comfort and/or satisfy him.

- *You establish your authority.* For some males, the first stage is most important; those who cherish Queen or Goddess fantasies love to stretch out this process. For others, such as males who prefer the Governess or Nursemaid fantasies, your establishment of authority may almost be taken for granted. Males with Amazon fantasies may go either way; some enjoy struggling with a Female who masters them, while others prefer to take the Lady's authority as read and get on with the second or even third stage.

    During this stage, you may set up the fantasy situation (you are a pirate Queen who has kidnapped him, and you wish to test his strength and stamina before deciding whether to sell him as a slave or keep him yourself; you are a Governess who Rules her charge with spankings and humiliation); snap out orders for him to obey; force him to dress, speak, move, and behave differently (as a sissy maid, a baby, or a schoolboy); deprive him of liberty by keeping him in bondage; or demand and receive maid service, body worship, oral servitude, or whatever you like. (Some submissives prefer to be rewarded with body worship and oral servitude at the end of the discipline session, rather than enjoying it unearned at the beginning. For more details, see the individual chapters on the five archetypal fantasies.)

This stage is exceedingly gratifying to the Mistress, and may indeed result in a number of sexual climaxes.

- *He transgresses.* Again, the duration and intensity of this stage vary with the type of fantasy. Submissives who seek the Governess or Queen archetypes may commit many tiny transgressions, each with its separate punishment, while those who desire a Goddess, Amazon, or Nursemaid may not actually commit a crime at all. In those fantasies, the submissive is punished – or rewarded – with pain at your whim.

  If you're playing with the idea of transgression, you must know precisely what infraction you are punishing him for, in order to scold him most effectively. But you don't actually have to catch him smoking, for example, to correct him for doing so. For some submissives, the only transgression is having been born male instead of being one of the superior sex.

- *You punish him.* This stage is the paramount one for many male submissives. Whether you spank him over your knee or punish his penis with a wire dog brush, the pain and humiliation he must undergo is crucial. Plan this stage carefully. Know how much pain he can take, what postures and toys he finds most embarrassing, and what kind of chastisement he needs. Then go to it with a will.

- *You comfort and/or satisfy him.* For some submissives, punishment itself (perhaps with accompanying tears) is the release; for others, the orgasm or consolation following the punishment is cathartic. Find out early what your submissive wants and needs, and be sure to supply it!

  After enduring the pain, the submissive may feel that he has earned the right to perform some intimate service for the Mistress: rendering obeisance to the Dominant's Shrine, for example, or bring permitted to rub her feet and polish her shoes. Take advantage of these tendencies, and not only because they provide you with pleasure. For some submissives, these tasks are essential rewards for having borne your rigorous discipline, bliss after agony. Males with Queen and Goddess fantasies are most likely to look on the comfort stage as the ultimate purpose of the discipline session, as opposed to the discipline itself. (See the chapters on individual fantasies for an explanation of the rewards each type of submissive is seeking.)

It is entirely your choice whether and how your submissive will obtain an orgasm at the end of the session. An orgasm is almost always the end of the session. Punish him and postpone the orgasm, and you will find him tractable again. You may, upon practice, to be able to extend the game indefinitely as long as your male doesn't climax.

Methods of orgasm vary; you may choose to permit your slave to masturbate or give him satisfaction with your hand, or you may end the session and move on to intercourse. Or for whatever reasons, neither you nor your sub may have a conventional orgasm. They are not compulsory.

Assemble Your Equipment

As you know from Chapter 5, setting the scene properly is essential to making a fantasy work. Once you have decided on a specific script, list all the equipment and clothing you will need to fulfill that script. Do you need any new items? Or can you use the toys you already have to fulfill the fantasy?

Buying Female Dominance equipment and clothing can be an erotic experience for both of you. If you visit stores, you can maintain your Dominance by commanding him to carry the items you select. (You can also make him wear satin panties or a chastity device beneath his street clothes, or, if he enjoys full-fledged cross-dressing, make him dress as a Girl.)

If you prefer to shop by mail or Internet, browse the available choices together; while you make the major decisions, you may allow him to choose a single toy from among, say, three possibilities you have indicated. Specialty websites and catalogues carry a wonderful range of implements, from the black leather accouterments of the Amazon to the frilly crinolines suitable for a sissy maid to canes, birches, and wooden hairbrushes.

If you already have a good many toys to choose from, you may wish to organize them by number. List each item on a separate 3x5 card, describing the name, size, color, and use of each toy. Then you can command your submissive to bring you number 34, 12, 17, and 3, and he will show up with the collar, leash, whip, and gloves you have designated. Some submissives find this powerfully erotic; fetching the implement of correction makes them shiver with anticipation. You may prefer to keep the mystery (and the power) by choosing and laying out the equipment yourself, merely commanding your sub to dress in the garments you have laid out on the bed and present himself to you immediately, bringing the hairbrush with him. (That's a command that will strike fear into his heart.)

Few things are as annoying in the midst of an intense session as reaching for an implement and finding that it's still in the closet, the cellar, or wherever you store your toys. Figure out all you will need and then make sure it is clean, handy, and ready for use. A disorganized Mistress loses half her authority.

Give Him Notice

How do you let your submissive know you are planning a scene? For that matter, how does he convey the idea that he needs one? These elementary issues of communication must be worked out, for many submissives feel resentful if they have to initiate Dominance play, while Mistresses grow angry when they wish for a scene and their male says no. The better your communication the rest of the time, the better this will be, but still you should work out a clear code.

Calling one another by your Dominance or submission name is an open invitation to a session. Or you could surprise your submissive by letting him come home from work or an errand to find you in full Dominance garb and his own submission clothing laid out, ready to wear. In either situation, however, you must always be willing to accept a no from him; he may be sick, exhausted, or simply not in the mood, and you must respect that. Likewise, he should be able to understand that you're not always ready to play, any more than you are always ready for sex or food or any other pleasure. It is no reflection on your Dominance to refuse him now and then.

You could also call him at work and leave a coded message. Even if he isn't in the mood at the moment he receives your note, anticipation may convert his other emotions into the lust to submit to you. If you use voice mail or E-mail, make sure the code is unbreakably innocuous. You don't want his whole law firm to hear or read about his crinoline and sissy panties. If he is dying for a session, he should be permitted to suggest it to you by the same means, and with the same caveats.

You might also schedule a regular time – Wednesday nights, for example, or the last weekend of each month – and always have a session then. The virtue of scheduling is that you both build up anticipation as the days go on, and you have a chance to plan and set the scene. You should, if at all possible, refuse other social obligations on your regular date night. (Your friends may or may not know precisely what you do on your dates, but they are certain to be impressed by your steady commitment to one another.) The disadvantage of this approach is that it doesn't work if either of you must travel unpredictably and alone on business.

The Great Safeword Debate

In giving your submissive notice that you will be disciplining him, you may also wish to remind him of the safeword. "Red" is good for "stop immediately, I'm in serious trouble"; "yellow" is often used for "please slow down, I'm starting to have a problem." The safeword does not mean your sub is giving you orders. He is giving you information – information you vitally need for a safe, sane, and consensual experience.

The safeword should always, always be instantly respected. If things are too intense, your submissive must be able to stop them; if you refuse to stop, he will lose his trust in you. And trust, as we saw back in Chapter 1, is one of the essential elements of successful Dominance/submission relationships.

A safeword is especially useful in Domestic Discipline situations, where your submissive wants to be free to struggle, resist, and moan, "No, please, stop!" in the full confidence that you will override his veto. If you do play this way – in a world where "no" means "more, more" – be sure you discuss it beforehand, and be prepared to deal with the fallout when you make a mistake.

However, the safeword is not a perfect guarantee that nothing will go wrong. Nor does a safeword relieve you of the obligation to make sure everything is all right with your submissive. You need to keep aware of his breathing, the temperature of his hands and feet (if he's in bondage), the expression on his face, and any other signs of trouble. Safewords fail sometimes, not because the sub refuses to use them (which is in fact a potential problem), but because he doesn't know things are going wrong. It's your responsibility to watch everything.

Also, sometimes a submissive is so deeply dived – so intensely involved in the fantasy – that he can't use the safeword to save his life. Some subs lose the power of speech when they are dived. Others become psychologically incapable of stopping you. So use a safeword if you feel more comfortable that way – but remember it is not infallible.

Act Out the Scene

And now, at last, the moment you've both been waiting for. The play itself. Yours may not – will not – follow this model exactly, but this is a fair representation of the ordinary script. It will at least set you to thinking how your scene could and should be different.

Act One: Dominatrix in Command. In the opening act, you must establish your authority. Using costumes, lighting, make-up, voice, and whatever lines are appropriate to the role you are playing, you must show your submissive that you are now in charge. (See Chapter 5 for specific suggestions on establishing your authority.)

He will almost certainly resist, although in some small way that seems apparently helpful and submissive. He might suggest that you tie him up in a certain way, that you use another instrument to punish him, or that he wear a specific costume.

Take note of the request for later use, but under no circumstances should you grant it! You must establish yourself as the protagonist in this little drama. Your ideas, your preferences, your will, are all that matter now. Tell him so.

Remind him that the safeword is "red" or whatever you have chosen, and that if the scene becomes too intense for him he may always use it. Unless and until he does, you are quite uninterested in his ideas and preferences. And if he does not do what you command, immediately, he will endure the consequences of your displeasure!

I cannot emphasize this point too strongly. If your submissive uses the safeword, by all means stop. You must; it's part of the contract between you. If he's obviously in trouble, you must stop. However, your authority is also in the contract, and you must maintain it, no matter what he does or says (short of the safeword) to test or undermine it. If you fail to assert your power now, your vassal will feel disappointed. He wants to test your limits and find them strict.

This is the point at which many prospective Mistresses fail. If you are not autocratic enough, but are too ready to please the male you should be controlling, neither of you will have a satisfying experience. He will feel cheated, as though he were secretly directing the whole scene, which is hardly what he desires. And you will feel powerless and angry. You tried to please him but he wasn't pleased.

Well, don't try to please him. Please yourself. Ultimately both of you will be happier.

Now that you have quelled his first stirrings toward rebellion, don't let the pace down. Hustle him into the next stage. A scolding, a change of clothes, whatever is the next logical step in the fantasy you have selected. Keep him moving. Remember the importance of the two kinds of suspense. Always keep the initiative in your hands.

If, as a Goddess or Queen-style Mistress, you use cunnilingus or another kind of service to establish your power, this is the moment to demand it. As a Nursemaid, you should be bundling your charge into his diapers and warning him about the potential consequences of his temper tantrums. If you are a Governess, you should be preparing your naughty male for the discipline he richly deserves: sending him to fetch a birch, pulling down his trousers, bending him over the chair, telling him how much the twigs will sting, and so forth. In an Amazon fantasy your slave should be bound now, while you begin to taunt and torment him. In all the fantasies, the stage is set for the second act: the discipline of your submissive male.

Act Two: Punishment. At this point, few submissives are feeling insubordinate. He is unlikely to defy you openly now (for defiance, after all, recognizes you as an authority with the right to command him) unless he wants a heavier castigation than he thinks he is likely to get. (Yes, you should give it to him.) Indeed, the naughty male is more likely to be seized with fright. He isn't sure he can take the punishment he has invited; he is certain, however, that he doesn't want to undergo it. He may appeal to you in your everyday persona, asking you not to do this, begging to end the fantasy. Harden your heart against these touching appeals. Unless he uses the safeword, he probably isn't serious. And yes, it's a matter of judgment.

Instead, respond in your Mistress persona, sharply commanding him to do as you say. If necessary, threaten to double his punishment unless he obeys you instantaneously. You may make various other threats: to reveal his wickedness to others if he doesn't comply, to forbid him ever to serve you again, or whatever best suits the fantasy.

Physical restraints, common in Amazon and Goddess fantasies, make continuing the scene easier. In a schoolboy or nursery fantasy, you may seize him by the hair or an ear and bend him over, punishing any struggles with a smart whack on the bottom. Sissy maids are less likely to rebel, but they do plead and whine. Simply continue with the planned punishment, despite tears and moans.

Remember that if he really wanted to end the scene, he would use the safeword. All the pleas and protests are simply a way to heighten his own arousal and reveal to you your own power: for, despite his begging, you are indeed going to punish him thoroughly. Once you have him in punishment position, you should play on his fear. The fear magnifies any punishment you bestow, making a simple spanking an experience of overwhelming power. Specific suggestions for dialogue are given in the chapters on individual fantasies.

Act Three: Denouement. Once he has been thoroughly punished, console him. Some submissive males (sissy maids, slaves of Amazons, and Goddess worshippers) may wish to be rewarded with a chance to give you pleasure or show their renewed devotion after the pain. Adult babies and schoolboys may have to spend time in the corner as part of their punishment, but afterwards they are eager to be petted and consoled, told how well they took their medicine, and questioned about how they plan to conduct themselves in the future.

Then, at last, the orgasm. The method of administering it depends so much upon the fantasy that generalizing becomes nearly impossible. Some males may achieve orgasm directly, via the chastisement; you should nevertheless console them afterward.

After the Scene

Once the scene is over, usually after the submissive has had an orgasm, you need a ritual to help you revert to your ordinary selves. Cleaning up and putting away the toys, hugging, perhaps discussing the scene (unless you prefer to wait a while) all can help you make the transition back to your normal selves. You may choose to play a special piece of music, share a pot of tea, or take a shower together. You could just be together silently, savoring your closeness, or you could take advantage of the extraordinary rapport to have a deep conversation. After a few sessions, you should be able to work out a routine that soothes you both.

There are a few potential problems immediately after a discipline session. You're both in a vulnerable state right now, and you need to be considerate of one another. However, you may find that you always argue, that your submissive starts viciously teasing, or that he icily withdraws from you. Any of these reactions may mean that one or both of you have problems dealing with the intimacy. Thus the impulse to shatter it rudely with an argument, a malicious criticism, or a cold put-down.

It could also indicate a problem with the scene itself, and you should discuss that thoroughly. Did it bring up old traumas? Does your submissive want a kind of play he isn't getting, or is getting exactly what he wants so overwhelming that he has to pull back from it? If you consistently argue after your scenes, consider seeing a couples therapist or stop playing out fantasies. You don't need to put up with nastiness (and, of course, you shouldn't be dishing it out, either).

Most couples, however, find that after a discipline session they feel more loving and committed than ever before. They have gone through an ordeal together, faced parts of themselves that most people never look at, and have come through with their mutual confidence and responsibility intact. There is no deeper trust.

7

THE ART OF DISCIPLINE:
Advice, Techniques, and Implements

"Use every man after his desert, and who should 'scape whipping?" –
Shakespeare, "Hamlet"

"Discipline," in the context of Domestic Discipline, almost always means spanking. Spankings may range from childish smackings to intense birchings, but all are chastisements inflicted on the buttocks, and the basic techniques are very similar. This chapter will teach you to choose and use the type of spanking, the implement, and the necessary force. Much of the advice here assumes that you are giving spankings in a play punishment context, in conjunction with roleplaying. However, if your sub is eager to enjoy spanking just for the sensation, or if you would rather dispense with the fiction of discipline, you will find plenty of useful techniques and ideas.

Although effective spanking is not the only discipline skill a Mistress needs, it is a truly useful one, applicable to almost every submissive, from the Nursemaid's adult infant to the Goddess's slave. The reasons, rituals, implements, and force may differ, but every variation of the Dominance experience includes the physical punishment of the submissive.

Basic Spanking Techniques

Where Should I Spank? No, we're not discussing the issue of public humiliation. Hard as it may seem to believe, we're discussing the proper place-ment of the spanking blows themselves. Each individual smack should fall where it will be both safe and erotic. Blows that fall upon bones, veins, organs, and joints are unerotic as well as dangerous.

Now you may be wondering whether any spot on the human frame is safe for chastisement. The answer is yes. The safest locations for punishment are also the most erotic location for punishment: the fleshy lower half of the buttocks, and the upper thighs. (Of course there are other kinds of punishment than spanking, but they will be dealt with in Chapter 8.) If you have any other spots in mind, go back and reread "A Necessary Warning" at the beginning of the book.

The buttocks are truly the dream spot for correction. Fleshy and full and ordinarily hidden, they are already a subject of no little embarrassment even without the threat of having them bared and beaten. Their proximity to a number of forbidden zones helps make them a seat (forgive the pun) of a sexually charged self-consciousness. The erotic feeling produced by shame is intensified by physiology: their nerves are intertwined with those of the genitalia. Altogether they are delightful and yet humiliating, a perfect venue for the mixture of both that makes Dominance so arousing.

The most forbidden and sensitive part of the bottom is the lower half, where the muscles are plumpest and the division between them is deepest. The "sweet spot," a spanker's delight, is the lower central portion of the buttocks, spreading generally from the crest of one nether cheek to the crest of the next. This spot, situated over and around the cleft, is highly susceptible to both painful and erotic sensations.

Any blows that land further out, toward the hips, have less impact than those that fall on this plump, quivering flesh. The spot where the buttocks round in to join the thighs is also delightfully impressionable. The backs of the thighs themselves must be struck with care; unless the submissive is unusually plump, bone and veins are often close to the surface here.

Although you need not place every smack in that magic zone, the sweet spot definitely deserves attention in your chastisements. If you are tempted to whip other spots, reasoning that your submissive is seeking pain and will appreciate your thoughtfulness, forget it. A stubbed toe is decidedly painful but not sexy. Raw pain is already too widely available in the world; a mixture of pleasure and pain, the goal of erotic punishment, is both rare and precious for the submissive.

The Two Types of Blows

There are two types of spanking blows, sting and thud. Sting is designed to stimulate the skin, while thud is intended to stimulate the deep muscles of the buttocks. The difference is partly a result of applied force, partly of implement, partly of aim.

Sting. In a stinging blow, you aim at the skin, using the strength of your forearm only, and you strike with fingers first or at the same time as the palm. You may splay your fingers to widen the area of impact. Sting may literally hurt the Mistress more than the submissive, so it is better to apply these blows with the back of a hairbrush or another implement. They are quite effective without doing deep damage: they sound dramatically loud, rapidly redden the bottom, provoke wriggling and yelling, and generally give the impression of a severe spanking without inflicting the pain of one.

The Deep Blow. The deep blow is a different story. You apply it by swinging your arm from the shoulder, and the palm lands first. Your aim is not the skin, but the deep muscle tissue of the bottom. You can – and should – swing your whole arm without using your full force. These deep blows make less noise than the stingers, but they set the cushion of the buttocks quivering with aftershocks (and soon quivering with pain). Reddening depends upon the individual; a quite deep spanking may include little color at the time but later show up as an array of bruises or a very sore bottom. A deep spanking also seems to provoke less wriggling, although yelling, moaning, and sobbing, even tears, may occur.

These two types of blows may be applied with the hand, the birch, the hairbrush, or any other spanking implement. Under the individual sections on each implement I explain which type of blow is more appropriate and how much force should be used.

Pacing the Blows

Now that you know where to place the blows and how to gauge their intensity, you must learn the next great lesson in giving a truly satisfying spanking: pacing the blows.

All punishment is a balance between intensity and duration. More intense pain should last less time; if you want to prolong the punishment, use less intense stimulation. If you start out the spanking by striking with all your force, your submissive will yell the safeword far sooner, and you both will end up feeling abused and unsatisfied. The more aroused your submissive is, the more pain he can take. Just being in the position of punishment, whatever that might be for the fantasy you share, is probably arousing to him, and if you have followed the instructions given in Chapters 5 and 6, he is in a considerable state of suspense as well. Nevertheless, start the spanking slowly. Save some of your strength for later. You'll need it.

Although every submissive differs in what he wants and needs, the following basic principles may be of some service in helping you administer a thorough licking to your submissive. Careful attention to these details will enable you to administer a more effective spanking and allow your submissive to enjoy a longer, more painful chastisement than he thought he could bear. And yes, the active word is enjoy; a long spanking can be exceedingly fulfilling to the submissive, bringing him not only physical release but psychological satisfaction as well.

Rhythm. Varying the weight, frequency, and placement of the blows keeps the submissive off-guard, so he cannot blot the pain from his mind. The first few smacks should be firm and crisp but not too deep. A few stinging slaps to start bringing up the color is a good idea. Watch his reactions; when he seems to be getting too satisfied with how well he is taking the punishment, startle him with a few deeper blows.

You may alternate cheeks, smack up and down the bottom, or follow a more random pattern. Repeatedly smacking the same spot may result in bruises, and certainly intensifies the pain. A more widespread coverage, reddening the bottom uniformly, allows you to stretch out the chastisement without overwhelming the submissive.

Speed. A slow pace is traditionally most appropriate to caning, strapping, switching, and birching. In these varieties of punishment the miscreant must often count the blows aloud as they fall. Since each one sears the buttocks with great force, a slow pace allows the submissive to feel the full, lingering impact of the stripe and let it ebb a little so he can begin to dread the next one. Of course, you need not let the implement dictate to you; you can perfectly well tease your sub with light, rapid taps of a cane or switch, followed by slower, more forceful blows.

On the other hand, a moderate to fast pace is more in keeping with the use of the hairbrush, the paddle, and the hand. Although the submissive may also have to count these blows, each one is less intense and should be followed up more rapidly in order to keep the flow of the punishment going.

A rapid spanking is most appropriate for hand or hairbrush; a quick, impulsive over-the-knee chastisement of the naughty boy may not last more than a few minutes, but can produce a stinging, tingling rear end and a better-behaved submissive.

Weight and Timing. As the spanking goes on, you may use heavier and heavier blows. By now your submissive is growing accustomed to the pain and is probably extremely aroused as well. Change the ratio of stinging smacks to deep blows to favor the latter. His buttocks should be brilliantly colored and he should be sobbing or moaning. You may finish the chastisement with a fast flurry of heavy blows, concentrating on the sweet spot, or (if this is a counted chastisement, such as birching or caning), continue even more slowly and give the last blow with extra force.

Intensifying the Punishment

When, how, and where you apply discipline can make a mild spanking seem more severe and thus more effective. The first principle is: To make a relatively mild spanking seem more intense, heighten the shame involved.

Fetching the Implement. Before the punishment commences, an implement of some kind must be fetched to use in the correction. If the miscreant is bound, he obviously cannot be expected to find and bring you a hairbrush. However, if at all feasible, you should insist that he fetch the rod with which he will be punished.

Take a strong, disciplinary stance, erect and angry, perhaps with your hands on your hips. Command your submissive to bring you the hairbrush (or whatever implement you have chosen) – immediately! – and wait for him to return, his head hanging in shame and fear as he hands you the dreaded device.

While your submissive is performing this embarrassing errand, his mind will be possessed by the thought of the coming punishment, voluptuously dwelling on every excruciating detail of having his bottom bared; your lecturing him as he lies exposed over your lap; the pain of the first blows; his fears that he might shame himself still further by wriggling, crying, or trying to escape the dreadful pain; and the aftermath of corner time, cock torture, or whatever you have chosen as the ideal way to finish off the discipline. Consequently, by the time he arrives with the implement he will be thoroughly psychologically prepared for correction.

Asking for Punishment. This step is not always appropriate, but it can be exceedingly effective in breaking a defiant slave's will and showing him the wisdom of surrendering to your superior Authority. As he hands you the rod, he should say, "Please punish me, Mistress. I know I have been naughty. Please spank [whip, birch, cane, or whatever] me until my bottom is red and sore, so I won't disobey you ever again."

Depending on the fantasy archetype you are enacting, you may change the wording to suit your situation. You may also wish to have him confess his particular crime in this little speech. However you do it, you should choose one form and stick to it. It will become a ritual as familiar and shaming as the punishment itself, and add immeasurably to both his suffering and his sense of security.

If he should refuse to ask for punishment, you must encourage him with a taste of discipline. A few swipes of the cane or smacks with a hairbrush may make your point. Occasionally your submissive will resist all the way through a serious chastisement. If he does, you must not let him off asking for the punishment! He is testing you, and you must make sure that he finds your Regime as strict and unbending as a solid wooden paddle. If you have to paddle him into tears before he asks for the punishment, so be it. The only possible exception is if he uses the safeword. Then you must stop the scene short and discuss what went wrong. But as long as he doesn't use the safeword, he wants to be overborne.

Clothing and Unclothing. Carefully chosen punishment garb can add deep humiliation to the sting in a submissive's nether cheeks. Simply taking a submissive over your knee is quite embarrassing for him; forcing him to wear ruffled sissy panties as well may make even a brief chastisement well-nigh unbearable. Dressing the submissive like a little boy or in Feminine clothing adds special shame to the experience of being corrected.

"Baring up" the culprit's bottom is highly recommended. Clothing provides physical protection from the weight of the blows and psychological protection from the weight of the humiliation. Pulling down trousers and underclothing can be made a ritual of extreme shame. The slow revealing of the naked bottom is a sensual pleasure for you, the Mistress, and a slow building-up of mingled fear and anticipation for your submissive.

Delaying Tactics. Once those buttocks are naked, revealing all their plump secrets, you may not wish to start spanking immediately. The longer the suspense, the deeper your slave's fear and the more effective the final chastisement. So you may wish to follow several delaying tactics, once that bottom is bare.

You can arrange the culprit in position, pull down his pants, and then commence a lengthy lecture on the fresh, pale buns which will so soon be toasted and tingling; linger lovingly over the sting and fire you will soon be spanking into that bottom, and point out how shameful this position is, for such a big boy to need such harsh, childish punishment. Dwell on his errors and the changes you expect to see in him. Remind him of the corner time still ahead, and how his poor bottom will ache for days. By now he should be writhing in frustration and fear. Tell him he ought to lie still now; he'll need all his energy to bounce under your stern paddle.

The Well-Prepared Bottom. You may also apply various salves, lotions, and other treatments to the buttocks. A damp bottom is more sensitive to pain than a dry one. You may choose to wallop your submissive straight out of the bath or shower, or apply towels wrung out in hot water to the target area.

Hand lotion, a mixture of glycerine and water, or a thin film of soapy lather also intensify the sting. You should be lecturing him while you slowly rub the solution onto the bottom.

To punish real naughtiness, rub a stinging salve (Tiger Balm, Heet, or Ben-Gay are good examples; you may also use oil of peppermint) over the affected area before the spanking is to commence. Then wait several minutes, allowing the salve to develop its characteristic fiery burn, before you add your own fiery burn. You may also paddle your submissive first and then prolong the agony with a generous application of these deep-muscle rubs.

Public Punishment. You might consider punishing him before other people, which is a humiliation deep enough to make the lightest smack resound in your submissive's mind like a full-fledged whipping. However, this technique should only be performed before people in the scene who have signified their willingness to witness the chastisement. You violate others' rights when you expose them to a sexual game they have not consented to. Furthermore, this technique is potentially explosive: you must discuss it with your slave before you try it.

You can, however, adapt the technique. A surreptitious smack on the submissive's buttocks, especially if he is wearing submission gear under regular clothes, can be both discreet and exciting. You may also pretend to be punishing him before others; during the spanking, tell him who else is present and watching his humiliation.

Talking. This suggestion brings us to one of the great techniques to enhance punishment: talking. Once your submissive is in the position of punishment, whether bound in place by physical ties or a healthy fear of your anger, you should begin to talk. Lecture him on how naughty he has been and remind him of what he has done to deserve your wrath. Describe the chastisement to come, lacing specific details of the punishment with threats that he will be getting the spanking of his life, that his poor naughty bottom will be so sore he won't sit down for a week, and the like.

The style of it changes with the fantasy, of course; an Amazon taunting her captive might emphasize the shame of such a strong man being flogged by a woman, while a Nursemaid is more likely to tell her charge that he is so naughty she simply must spank his wicked little heinie until it's red and sore.

During the chastisement, you might want to pause and comment on the damage being done. The heat, color, and welts of the bottom should be emphasized or even exaggerated. You could ask for confessions of further wrongdoing (which will instantly entail extra punishment) or inquire whether the submissive is sorry for disobeying you. You might even ask if he has had enough, and then, when he says yes (as long as he doesn't use the safeword), laugh and tell him that you will judge when he has been punished enough, and then go on with the chastisement.

Combined Corrections. One of the best ways to intensify a discipline session is to combine two or more punishments. You may follow a hand spanking with the use of one of the inflexible implements (hairbrush or paddle), or use one of the flexible implements upon a bottom already prepared by a hand spanking or the use of a hairbrush or paddle. Warming the bottom thoroughly before using the sterner implements will intensify their sting and provide a delightful contrast between the broader coverage of hand or hairbrush and the more focused sensation of strap, switch, or birch. In cases of stubborn and repeated naughtiness, you may start the session with a hand spanking, move on to hairbrush or paddle, and crown the whole with a dozen strokes of the birch, switch, or cane.

Kissing the Rod. Whatever implement you choose, do not omit this ceremony! Kissing the implement that has just reduced him to nursery status and evoked tears, squirms, and other undignified behavior has the bitterness of utter abjection for the submissive male. But, just as he must fetch the rod and ask for punishment, he must kiss it afterwards and thank you sincerely for giving him the correction he needed and deserved.

Once again, choose a form for this ritual and stick with it. Its familiarity will make him feel comforted and secure, while the repeated words will deepen his humiliation every time he speaks them, reminding him not only of the current punishment (from which his bottom is still sore and glowing) but of all the ones that preceded it. He should kiss the rod and say, "Thank you, Mistress, for spanking [caning, birching, or whatever] me. I know I deserved it, and I'm sorry you had to punish such a big boy. Please forgive me, and make sure to punish me whenever you think I need it."

Should he refuse to perform this ceremony, the punishment is clearly not finished, for he has not surrendered completely to your authority. Return him to punishment position and give him a further dose until he indicates his willingness to kiss the rod.

"Kissing the rod" might seem impossible in a hand spanking, but it is not. You may choose to have him kiss your hand, or perhaps your cheek or foot, after which he must recite the apology.

Aftermath. After the punishment is over, your task is not done. You may wish to send a childish submissive to stand in a corner to display his bare, reddened nether cheeks and think about his crimes. (No rubbing of the affected parts should be permitted.) A sissy maid might be forced into various embarrassing postures or oral servitude. The slave of an Amazon or Goddess could stay in bondage or be forced to perform body worship. Once these things are done, you may forgive your submissive, allow him to have an orgasm, and end the scene.

Using Pain Wisely

The novice Dominatrix, taken in by books, videos, and perhaps other Ladies' bragging, may feel it incumbent upon her to punish her submissive until he cries real tears. She may lash away at her bound slave, relishing the delightful exertion of her Authority, without realizing that he has long since stopped enjoying the punishment. (Of course, he should use the safeword, but he may not.) Few issues cause so much frustration, blame, and anger.

How does a responsible Mistress maintain strict discipline without inflicting severe chastisement? What is the line between erotic and discipline spankings? What do those blows actually feel like? When is enough enough, and how can you tell?

The Psychology of Punishment

By punishing your submissive, you establish and enforce your Authority over both his body and his mind. During a discipline session, your vassal knows unmistakably that you are in command and he is subordinate. But even in the midst of actual chastisement, the pain is not the essential element of your Dominance. Psychological factors far outweigh the sting of even the severest beating.

For example, a bare-bottomed, over-the-knee spanking derives much of its effectiveness not from the physical pain involved (which can range from negligible to intense, depending on duration, implement, and applied force), but from its sheer childishness. It is humiliating to be so treated, especially if the Mistress emphasizes the bare bottom, the embarrassing posture, and the naughtiness and immaturity of the howling, kicking male over her lap.

A wise Mistress takes advantage of these psychological factors to intensify and focus the pain she does inflict. The punishment should be chosen with the culprit in mind. What fantasies does he indulge in? What most bothers him? How can he be most effectively disciplined? What treatment does he need now to remind him of your power? Will humiliation add to his corporeal suffering? Can special clothing, posture, or audience heighten his embarrassment?

These considerations impart an extra sting to the submissive's already humiliating experience, yet they are truly kind. For without them, the Mistress might need to assert her Authority in far more severe and excruciating ways. And remember, he needs your ministrations, even the ones that leave bruises and soreness behind.

Erotic Versus Discipline Spankings. The topic of erotic spankings versus discipline spankings is a tangled and controversial one. At least in the Domestic Discipline world, erotic spankings almost all take place under the guise of discipline, while discipline spankings often contain a strong flavor of the erotic. Yet the distinction may be crucial to how you deal with the individual chastisement, not to mention your submissive.

Discussing the issue with your submissive (not during a session, of course) may or may not be helpful. A submissive is likely to claim in all honesty that he wants severe discipline spankings, and in a sense he probably does. He wants to feel as helpless and totally Dominated as a child being whipped. But he may also want it not to hurt so much that he loses his erection. No matter what the dialogue, the ostensible reason, the control you have over him, that is the deciding line. If he wants and needs a discipline spanking – and many submissives do, at least occasionally – he must be willing to suffer it without an erection. (Afterwards, of course, he will probably spring to full and throbbing life, but not during.) Some well-known Mistresses administer discipline spankings after the submissive has had an orgasm, effectively removing any erotic element from the punishment.

Discipline spankings tend to be extremely intense, at least psychologically. The exchange of power is almost overwhelming. Many couples who do discipline spankings don't use a safeword, since the point of a discipline spanking is that the Dominant knows what is best for the submissive and can be trusted to punish without doing lasting harm. To be honest, discipline spankings tend to be the province of couples who have been involved in the scene a long time, who have tested their limits together for years. Both may have played with others and have a clear and confident understanding of the physiology and psychology of punishment. In short, this is no game for novices. Work your way up to discipline spankings gradually.

A good erotic spanking counterfeits the discipline version, while leaving the submissive more independence. A skillful Mistress can make the illusion seem complete without stirring the murky psychological depths of true punishment. In both kinds of spanking, the Dominatrix must constantly and carefully observe her submissive, checking his physical reactions and his emotional state. But an erotic spanking, painful as it may be, is never too much to bear.

Experiencing a Spanking. No book, movie, fantasy, or friend can tell you what a spanking feels like. You have to learn the dreads and delights of that practice over someone's knee. All good Dommes test new implements on their own flesh – swatting a thigh, a calf, a forearm to feel the weight and character of the toy. But even that won't tell you what a submissive experiences. In some ways, the best Mistress may be the switch: a Woman who understands submission as well as Domination because she practices or has practiced both. When she inflicts a bare-bottom spanking, she knows how the shame and the pain must feel; she has experienced them. If you have never been a switch, you might consider finding someone to administer a sound spanking to you, on the principle that experience will teach you far better than theory ever could just what you are doing (and how to make improve your technique) when you paddle a submissive's fanny.

You may decide to switch with your submissive, or, if that idea fails to appeal, seek out a Mistress or male dominant to handle you. Indeed, some experienced Mistresses, committed believers in Female Rule who would never dream of permitting their submissive to take the reins for even an hour, regularly schedule time with a fellow Mistress in which they can balance their power with a dose of submission and punishment. Then, feeling cleansed and peaceful from the discipline, they return refreshed to the Rule over males that so deeply satisfies them.

When He's Had Enough. How much punishment is enough? There is no single answer; it varies with your submissive's tolerance levels, the intensity of the scenario, and the degree to which he has sinned. Start with less pain; you can always add more as you watch his reactions. This is one of the issues you must discuss beforehand, but even hours of conversation will not inform you of his exact need for and tolerance of pain. You must watch his reactions, remain open to his needs, and control yourself. Going too far may turn him off to your Rule for good.

Specifically, watch for the following signs that your punishment is working. At the beginning of the chastisement your submissive may try to be manly, stoic, and silent. He could even be openly defiant of your authority, saying outrageous things to spur you on. He might wriggle and try to escape.

You are getting through to him when he starts to make noise. He may plead, moan, or sob (make crying noises without tears). If he is still struggling with your authority, however, trying to crawl off your lap or escape the ropes, you should probably keep on. Submission is often revealed by lying still and accepting the blows. You don't need to push him to the point of tears to have earned his submission.

Physical signs that the spanking has gone on too long include splotchiness of the buttocks, then pimpling or blistering. If you keep on striking him after his bottom has started to pimple, he could start to bleed. That is far too severe a punishment. If you use a cane, a switch, or a birch, you may have wealing; you could even draw blood if you are not careful with these precision implements. Most submissives do not need, want, or like to be punished to this extent.

You and your sub may prefer to end the chastisement before you've done damage that will mottle his bottom for a week. Remember, the better you are at creating suspense, the less actual physical pain you need to inflict on your submissive. But won't he be disappointed if he doesn't get all the pain he wants? Perhaps a little, but if you give him all the drama he needs, he may not even notice that you didn't push him to his physical limits.

Implements of Correction

Discipline may be administered with a number of implements, some formal, some improvised. They fall into three categories: the human hand, rigid implements, and flexible implements. Rigid implements include paddles, hairbrushes, and wooden spoons. Flexible implements include straps, canes, birches, and the various sorts of whip. Each type has its own etiquette of use: the rating of severity, the culprit's position, and the fantasies that best display its unique virtues.

The Human Hand. No other spanking implement offers the range, delicacy, and precision of this most perfect instrument. Hand and bottom might have been expressly designed for one another. Furthermore, this instrument, with its echoes of childhood and a Mama's stern affection, may melt a slave's rebellious heart when a whip or a cane would harden his defiance.

Spankings with the hand may be mild smackings, more notable for the shame they produce than any excess of pain, or they may be more severe, tiring the Disciplinarienne and producing tears and genuine soreness in the spankee. Because the very nature of the hand makes permanent damage impossible, as long as it is applied only to the fundament, a physically severe punishment is less likely to occur when the Mistress uses her hand only. Nevertheless, the psychological severity of the punishment may be great, especially if the spanking is given in especially shaming circumstances: in public, for example, or wearing punishment clothing. Remember, the more humiliating the punishment, the less pain you need to get your point across.

The very intimacy of the hand spanking – and this is the most intimate of all punishments – makes for additional shame, yet the closeness of Mistress and male acts paradoxically as a comfort and a consolation to him, assuring him all through the pain and humiliation that the chastisement is indeed for his own good, not just a cruel whim of an uncaring Dominatrix, but the sorrowful correction of an angry but loving Lady. Consequently, the best fantasies for this practice are the domestic archetypes: the Nursemaid, Governess, and Queen fantasies.

The culprit may be held over the knee, over the lap, or under the MIstress's arm, with the Mistress standing. Keep one hand firmly on the submissive's back, holding him down, while you belabor him with the other. One or both the lad's legs may be clamped between your thighs to prevent escape. You may be seated on a straight chair or, to help spread the submissive's weight, on the edge of a bed, with the naughty one lying upturned over her lap. All of these positions present the nether cheeks in a way lusciously inviting to the Mistress's hand.

More than any other punishment, the pacing and weight of the hand spanking depend on the situation. What fantasy are you enacting? What crime has the naughty boy committed? How seriously should he be punished? In general, hand spankings should be paced at a moderate to quick rate; blows may be light, medium, heavy, or a variety. Spank until your submissive whimpers or cries, until he shows the deep contrition you expect, or halt the spanking when the target area is blushing brightly and move on to the hairbrush, the strap, or even the switch.

Few discipline scenes are as heartwarming as the intimate grouping of a Mistress with her submissive over her knee, getting the fan-tailing he needs and deserves. The rich color staining his nether cheeks, the flurry of smacks followed by sobs and whimpers, the stern look on her face and the shamed expression on his—all add up to a magical moment in discipline.

The Hairbrush. The wooden hairbrush is one of the great traditional spanking implements. It may be purchased from specialty stores, although many bath and body shops now sell fine wooden brushes sizes ranging from the tiny (for cleansing the face), to the full-size hairbrush, to lengthy monsters designed for scrubbing the back but useful lower down as well. The weight and smoothness of the wooden back help make this implement effective, and its size makes it both portable and easily directed to the most sensitive portions of the masculine buttocks. But the real mystique of the hairbrush is its Femininity. An implement so intimately connected with Female rituals of grooming is bound to carry some fascination for submissive males; its connection to Female rituals of discipline nearly drives them wild.

A hairbrush spanking uses the same positions as the hand spanking and maintains much of the sweet intimacy that adds such charm to hand spanking. Yet it can be much more severe, causing bruising if the blows are too vigorous or the punishment goes on too long. A good, thorough hairbrush spanking may consist of one hundred to two hundred moderate smacks on the nether cheeks. If you choose to use more force, twenty to fifty may be more than enough. A light hairbrush spanking may go on almost indefinitely. Remember the rule: All punishment is a balance between intensity and duration.

The hairbrush is best suited to moderate and severe punishments, because the hard wooden surface allows you to continue smacking long after your hand would have tired. You may wish to save it for especially intense sessions or particularly heinous crimes, especially if you are using it on an adult infant. Schoolboys and sissy maids can take more punishment. The hairbrush is extraordinarily suitable to the sissy maid: it is one of the few implements that can be used with painful effect over a pair of ruffled panties without doing them any damage. It also plays well into the fantasy of a stern Queen punishing a clumsy or insolent servant.

The Wooden Spoon. Although a minor instrument, the wooden spoon deserves at least a glance before we move on to the rigors of the paddle, the strap, and the switch. The charm of the spoon, which functions very much like a hairbrush, is its intimacy, its sweet spontaneity, and its domestic nature. It is an implement seized in the heat of the moment to be used upon a miscreant with no loss of time.

The culprit may be standing, pulled roughly over the Mistress's knee, or tucked under her arm, and the spoon should be used with great speed and energy.

A wooden spoon may be applied with vigor without producing serious harm because it is relatively light in weight. It is most suitable for Nursemaid and Governess fantasies.

The Paddle. The heavy paddle of schooldays still has its uses in adult life. It may give a moderate to severe spanking, either in the relative intimacy of Queen and sissy maid or the remoteness of Goddess and votary. The familiar wooden paddle (appropriate for use by Governesses and sometimes Queens) is widely available through specialty stores and, in some unenlightened states, teacher supply stores. It may also be purchased quite cheaply as a souvenir from various tourist destinations, often emblazoned with one of several embarrassing sayings. The leather paddle (more suitable to sterner Queens, Amazons, and Goddesses) is always on display at specialty stores and can be mail-ordered.

Whether the Disciplinarienne is a Governess or a Goddess, she forces her submissive into the same humiliating position to accept this punishment. She bends him over the back of a chair, with the edge coming just at the level of his hip joints, so his fundament is best displayed. If necessary or desirable, he could be standing on tiptoe. Or she may bend him in a similar pose over a desk. Either position tightens the buttocks and makes each smack more painful. Naturally, the naughty male's buttocks should be bared for this punishment. You should see precisely what color your paddle is lending those nether cheeks.

You should start a paddling using a moderate pace and a light-to-medium stinging stroke. As the punishment continues, you may use heavier, deeper strokes; notice as you paddle that these strokes naturally come more and more slowly. The last few blows should be quite slow and heavy, although some Mistresses prefer finishing up with a flurry of rapid, stinging smacks to bring up a fresh, bright color. A dozen smacks should be considered the minimum to bring the buttocks into a fine, well-spanked glow. More smacks may be administered as needed, of course.

The Strap. The leather strap (or strop, or belt) may be a fearsome instrument, but it is exceedingly useful in the discipline of many types of submissive. No adult infant should be punished with a strap, but all other submissive males should be made aware that they are subject to this stern, traditional form of discipline.

Straps are nearly all made of leather; they vary in length, thickness, flexibility, width, and surface texture. The wider the strap, the more broadly the pain is distributed; the narrow strap is a severe instrument indeed. Long or flexible straps may be folded to provide extra spring and force to the blows. Smooth leather is faster and whippier than suede, which clings more to the punished buttocks.

Old-fashioned razor strops, which are relatively stiff and thick, provide a high degree of discipline; they may sometimes be purchased in antique stores or in specialty Victorian catalogues. Specialty stores sell a wide array of straps, from viciously narrow ones to broad, studded monsters. (Never use a studded strap for discipline. They may cause injury. Use them for decoration or bondage only.) The tawse is a thick leather strap cut into two or three fingers at the business end, giving it truly extraordinary bite. Since it was designed for the naughty bottoms of Scottish schoolgirls, any male submissive feels especially humiliated by this "Feminine" implement.

Instead of purchasing a specialty item, you may wish to begin your career as a strapping Mistress with a visit to a thrift shop, where you are likely to find leather belts of many interesting lengths, colors, and textures. Look for the braided belts so popular a few years ago; they are ideal instruments for topping up a strapping with a plain belt. Those last two or three blows with the braid really give the miscreant something to think about! However, do not discount the power of a simple leather belt. Its good effects may be viewed for days after the punishment. Remember to remove the buckle first to prevent any chance of serious injury.

The strap, properly applied, is really more severe than moderate in effect. Although an old-fashioned form of punishment suitable to grown schoolboys, naughty farm lads, and other domestic fantasies, it is severe and distant enough to be used by a Goddess. As we have already demonstrated, it comes in enough various forms to satisfy both the high-style Amazon and the simple country Schoolmarm.

The submissive to be punished may take any of a number of intriguing postures for his punishment. The classic positions described for a paddling or a hand spanking may be used, although any strapping done over the knee must be done with a doubled strap. Any bent-over position – grabbing the ankles, bent over a bathtub after a shower, gripping the far edge of a desk – is useful. However, the strap is uniquely suited to a posture that rarely works for any other implement. Bare up the naughty submissive and make him lie face-down across a bed. Prop up his buttocks with pillows underneath him, so that the target is appetizingly presented as a high mound. If the submissive is resisting punishment, you may tie his hands and feet to the bedposts. Then get to work.

Give him a dozen to start with, using a deliberate pace and light to medium blows. The first few should be stingers aimed at the skin; then move on to deeper smacks, aiming at the fleshy underbottom. That may very well be plenty of punishment; if not, add a few more until your submissive has surrendered to the punishment. Be careful of bruising and blistering.

The strap is so severe that it may be used as an extra punishment after a spanking with hand or hairbrush. In that case, you should definitely announce the number of strokes you plan to give – six, eight, or twelve – and make your submissive count them aloud as you deliver each one. Add one extra stroke for losing count, two or more for resistance. Using the strap in combination is more effective than using it alone; it adds a dreadful dimension to the threat of a spanking, since the submissive knows if he doesn't take it well, resists, or tries to cover the target area with his hands, you will not hesitate to bring out the strap and give him a real walloping. Using the strap alone may make him fear it less.

The Switch. The switch is a pastoral implement available on almost any tree. The most popular switches are cut from birch (a special case; see below), peach (or other fruit trees), hickory, and willow. Birch switches, bundled together, make the Queen of all implements, the birch, but even a single length of birch, stripped of its twigs and leaves, makes a lasting impression on a naughty backside. Peach-tree switches have the flavor of the Old South, having been used on naughty Southern lads from colonial times even up to today. However, even a Yankee Governess may applaud their flexibility and sternness. The hickory switch is also a traditional favorite, from its toughness and durability; it is an excellent choice for lengthy punishments. Finally, the willow switch is more like a whip than a switch. Narrow and springy, it has the same effect as a lash.

The switch may be applied by the Governess, Queen, Amazon, or Goddess, though it is most used by the Governess and Queen.

Switches must be cut on demand, as they rapidly lose their suppleness and become dry and brittle. Sending a naughty submissive outside to choose and cut his own switch is an additional and humiliating punishment. Make him cut half a dozen, so you may choose the most supple and strong from among them. You should always have at least one spare, in case the original breaks.

Position the culprit in one of the traditional bent-over postures: grabbing his ankles or supported by the back of a chair or a desk. You should stand on his left side (assuming you are right-handed; on the right if you are a lefty), so that his buttocks are in profile to you, and a heart-lifting sight they will be, so full, tight, and round, and so fair and white before the first touch of the switch. In a few moments they will be red and stinging, with long slim lines across to underscore your submissive's naughtiness. You might wish to tell him so before you begin the chastisement.

Then apply the switch, being careful to watch how the light, flexible ends bite into the further flank. With practice, you can control the whippiness of the switch, choosing to apply so that it falls all at once across the bottom, or rolling it a little so that it bites in on the near side first, then curls into the farther side. Use a slow pace and a light to medium force, mingling stingers with one or two deeper cuts. Especially if you have already prepared him with a thorough hand-spanking or hairbrushing, he will soon be jumping at the thin, intense pain of the stripes across his nether cheeks. Let the rod do the punishing; you need not back the strokes with the full weight of your arm. Indeed, some experts advise that you use the arm only from the elbow down.

Make him count the strokes. In most cases, a dozen moderate stripes will do, especially if the bottom has already been prepared by a good spanking. In severe cases you may give up to two dozen.

The rural charm of the switch may be best displayed on picnics. In a secluded grove on private property, have your submissive cut a selection of switches from various trees. The process of testing them on his bare bottom would be sufficiently exhilarating even indoors, but to do so in the fresh outdoor air is especially exciting.

The Cane. The cane is superficially similar to the switch; indeed, both are narrow, flexible wooden rods, and the same positions are used for both. But if the switch is a delightfully pastoral, American instrument, suitable for spontaneous use alfresco as well as schoolroom situations, the cane is the most English implement available, with all the formal ceremony that description entails. The switch is available wherever a tree grows, but the cane must be purchased from a specialty shop.

Traditional canes are made of flexible rattan or malacca and two to three feet in length. The longer canes are considerably less easy to control; they tend to cut in, wrapping round the hips in an undesirable fashion, causing a kind of pain that is not in the least erotic.

Canes made of artificial materials are now available; I have a formidable armory of canes made from clear lucite, thin whippy delrin, fat thuddy delrin, narrow inflexible carbon fiber, and, of course, rattan. Thin whippy canes should be used more like a switch, while fatter, thuddier canes are much less likely to wrap.

The essence of good caning is control: placing the strokes in precise parallel lines on the fleshy underbottom. Random strokes lessen the effect. Practice using the cane on a pillow or sofa until you have it under control.

There are at least two styles of caning: the traditional or English style, which I have seen used in this country mostly by Domestic Discipline enthusiasts, and the Leather style. Naturally there are a thousand gradations, but the difference between the two styles is considerable.

- *Traditional English Caning.* This is a punishment so severe as to be well beyond most subs' limits. The point of the exercise is not a long, slow erotic warming, finishing with intensity. It is pain, pure and simple, and it hurts like hell.

   Because of the severity and intensity of the cane, the ritual that leads up to its use is especially important. You can only give your submissive six to twelve strokes, so each must carry a great deal of meaning. Furthermore, the pain is so great that only a well-prepared submissive can bear it. The Governess most often uses the cane in situations of repeated disobedience; although the Queen, the Amazon, and Goddess may sometimes use it, it is essentially a British schoolroom fantasy.

   Position the culprit in one of the traditional bent-over postures: grabbing his ankles or supported by the back of a chair or a desk. You should stand on his left side (assuming you are right-handed; on the right if you are a lefty), so that his buttocks are in profile to you. Warn him that he must keep his bottom open and relaxed for every stroke. He must take this punishment like a man, with no begging or pleading. Announce the number of strokes you intend to apply: four or six for ordinary offenses, with perhaps one extra if he loses count and another extra for clenching the buttocks.

Swinging from the shoulder or the elbow, wallop his ass hard with the cane, leaving thirty to sixty seconds between counted strokes. Wrapping is expected and unavoidable. If done by an expert, this apparently simple movement can leave welts that last for weeks. This is the sort of caning often featured in fiction, and in real life it is extreme.

Make him count the strokes. In most cases, four to six moderate stripes will do, especially if the bottom has already been prepared by a good spanking. In severe cases you may give up to one dozen strokes, maximum.

Afterward, you may expect to see red or purplish bruises on the buttocks, following the line of your strokes. Quite literally, the gentleman may not sit down comfortably for a week. If you prefer not to punish him so harshly, you may give the flavor of a caning by using light strokes following all the ritual outlined here, with perhaps a single moderate stroke at the end of the punishment. Even a mild English-style caning is an experience to remember.

- *Leather-style Caning.* The fearsome bite of the cane does not have to be used with punitive force. By using a light to medium weight, mingling surface blows with one or two deeper cuts, you can do a prolonged and pleasurably painful caning scene without leaving weeks' worth of welts. Let the rod do the punishing; you need not back the strokes with the full weight of your arm. Indeed, some experts advise that you use the arm only from the elbow down.

The Birch. The birch is the Queen of rods: a long, slim bundle of fresh or pickled birch, tied artistically with ribbons, and applied to a bare and blushing bottom. Its severity may be gauged by the fact that it was deemed too cruel an instrument in British schools, and therefore was replaced by the cane! A birch may be purchased through specialty shops or made up at home.

If you cut your own birch, choose half a dozen branches of two to three feet in length. Strip off the leaves and any dead, brittle twigs, leaving the main stem and all the smaller twigs. The branches will curve in one direction or other; arrange the bundle so that all curve inward, and trim the handle end so that all rods are of the same length. You may wrap the ends with florist's wire or electrical tape (which I prefer for its smoothness, elasticity, and superior coverage) to make a six- to eight-inch handle. Cover the wrappings well with cross-tied ribbons; classically, only one color was used, but I like a two-toned effect, crossing pink with lavender or pale blue with pale yellow.

The birch offers broader coverage than the cane, but produces an intense sting like no other implement. Six to twelve strokes are plenty for most subs. Because of the severity and intensity of the birch, the ritual that leads up to its use is especially important. The Governess, the Queen, the Amazon, and the Goddess may all use the birch, but it, like the cane, is at heart a British schoolroom fantasy.

Position the culprit in one of the traditional bent-over postures: grabbing his ankles or supported by the back of a chair or a desk. You should stand on his left side (assuming you are right-handed; on the right if you are a lefty), so that his buttocks are in profile to you. Warn him that he must keep his bottom open and relaxed for every stroke. He must take this punishment like a man, with no begging or pleading. Announce the number of strokes you intend to apply: four or six for ordinary offenses, with perhaps one extra if he loses count and another extra for clenching the buttocks.

Then apply the birch, swishing it in the air a few times to frighten him before you actually make contact. Leave thirty to sixty seconds between counted strokes. Use a light to medium force, mingling stingers with one or two deeper cuts. Let the rod do the punishing; you need not back the strokes with the full weight of your arm. Indeed, some experts advise that you use the arm only from the elbow down. Be especially careful about strokes that bite in. A prolonged or forceful birching may break the skin.

Make him count the strokes. In most cases, four to six moderate blows will punish him thoroughly, especially if the bottom has already been prepared by a good spanking. In severe cases you may give up to one dozen strokes, maximum.

Afterward, you may expect to see many fine, thin red or purplish bruises on the buttocks. Quite literally, the gentleman may not sit down comfortably for a week. If you prefer not to punish him so harshly, you may give the flavor of a birching by using very light strokes following all the ritual outlined here, with perhaps a single moderate stroke at the end of the punishment. Even a mild birching is an experience to remember. A severe one is too much for most submissives to bear.

Whips, Floggers, Cats. The whips, floggers, and cats are not really classic Domestic Discipline implements, but they can nevertheless be wonderful toys. Floggers in particular are a whole luscious kink in themselves.

Whips – usually known as singletails in the Leather community – are long, straight, flexible leather braids. Although the riding crop, a shirt, thick whip, may be used like a cane, the bullwhip made famous by Indiana Jones is difficult to use. You need a lot of room to swing a singletail properly, and you must understand that they are not to be used as a paddle, but to flick or brush the skin. There is no way I can teach you how to throw a singletail on paper. If you're interested in learning the proper stance and technique, find a demo or a skilled player and ask to learn. And for an exquisite display of artistry with a singletail, look for

Anthony Hopkins in "The Mask of Zorro" – a very hot movie that also includes a fireplay/furniture scene that made me weak in the knees.

The cat-o'-nine-tails is a bundle of braided leather lashes gathered and held together by a handle. It may be used like a birch, with less force, or as a flogger. The miniature version, only a foot or so long, may be lightly and playfully flicked over the penis and balls during cock torture. Never strike this area using anything but the lightest force! Think love pat, not smack or lash.

The flogger is made like a cat but with flat leather or suede falls, and it is truly one of the most sensual of all toys, with a powerfully erotic scent, feel, and motion. A good flogger may cost $150 or more. Less expensive ones may be well made, but there are plenty of chintzy floggers that can damage your technique. You ought to test the flogger first before buying, or else buy from a craftswoman (almost all the great flogger-makers are women) whose wares suit your taste.

Again, the proper stance, grip, and technique are essential, and best learned by direct apprenticeship. Floggers may be used as paddles, or to brush against the upper back of a bound, standing sub. I strongly recommend learning their use, though they are rarely used in a purely Domestic Discipline scene.

If you are a Queen, Amazon, or Goddess, you may decide that the symbolic importance of the whip (in the form of the riding crop) and the cat is so great that you must use them. If you do, follow the rules carefully. The crop should be administered with the same precautions as the cane; the birch should be the model for the use of the cat.

A Few Words in Conclusion

The art of discipline does indeed include the actual impact of an instrument upon the taut buttocks of the male submissive. But the most important part of discipline is the drama and ritual in which you embed it. Remember, pain alone is hardly satisfying. (No male gets an erection from a toothache.) The pain should be a natural extension of your authority and power, as well as a stimulation to the deep muscles of his buttocks.

8

THE SKILLS OF A MISTRESS:
Bondage, Humiliation, and Other Forms of Control

"The Good Life is waiting for us here and now!... At this very moment we have the necessary techniques, both material and psychological, to create a full and satisfying life for everyone." – B.F. Skinner, "Walden Two"

Whether you are an affectionate Nursemaid or a stern Amazon, you need certain skills for the restraint and discipline of rebellious males. The arts of correction have already been set forth in exquisite detail, but chastisement is not the only – or always the best – technique for keeping a submissive in line. This chapter discusses various other methods for controlling a submissive, including coercion, bondage, chastity devices, nipple stimulation, verbal humiliation, and the enema. It concludes with a delightful passage on how to maintain control of your submissive while you are in the throes of ecstasy – a skill which, I assure you, is exceedingly useful and pleasant to exercise.

Coercion

Physical coercion has earned a bad name in many circles, and indeed, it is not appropriate in dealing with dilatory workmen, venal politicians, stubborn children, heartless landlords, incompetent employers, lazy employees, or other annoying beings, however tempted you may be. Nevertheless, it has a place in handling the adult male submissive (and may be used to punish any of the irritating behaviors listed above, if you so desire). Coercion in this context includes all those means by which you, the Mistress, force the male into positions of humiliation, bondage, or punishment, or gain control of him when he has rebelled against your Authority. (Any such rebellion must be followed by instant and severe punishment, of course.)

The techniques listed here cause no permanent damage but make it difficult for the submissive to resist your will. Some are especially humiliating and childish, but that is all to the good.

Seize him by the ear. Holding a submissive by this sensitive spot enables the Mistress to lead him to punishment. A firm grip on the upper part of the ear is both painful and practical; it is, moreover, difficult to break such a grasp. He will march along quite willingly when you use this technique.

Tug him by the hair. The scalp is even more sensitive than the ear. By twining your fingers securely in his hair, you will get a good grip and be able to control his movements. If the male is much taller than you are, use this grip to bring him to his knees. Forcing a male to cross a room on his knees, traveling painfully toward deserved and severe chastisement, is quite thrilling for the Mistress.

Bend a finger. A subtle yet delicious way of forcing a male to do your bidding is to seize a finger – middle and ring fingers are generally most sensitive – bend it at the large central knuckle, and squeeze. This action forces the outermost part against the hand and is surprisingly painful. (Try it out on yourself to understand the technique and the sensation.)

You may also bend back a finger or two, but this procedure is riskier. Do not break his finger. Fractures are unerotic.

Grip his male member. Glaringly unsubtle but effective. As a great government official once expressed it, "If you've got them by the balls, their hearts and minds will follow."

Methods differ depending on whether the male is in a state of sexual arousal. If he is not erect, you may seize and twist his member or even the scrotum. Grasp the sac from below, placing your fingertips just atop the testicles, and twist one-half turn. This technique, amazingly similar to the preferred way to seal bread in a plastic bag, moves the skin, making the balls bulge within a suddenly smaller sac. Under this compulsion, your slave will follow wherever you lead.

If he is erect, a solid grip on penis enables you to lead him, or you may choose to encircle the base of the scrotum and the engorged member with your fingers. No matter what his size, you should be able to make your thumb and forefinger meet around them. Then you may deal with him as you please. Gentle pressure of a few fingers on one testicle is generally enough to make him do exactly as you say.

As always when dealing with the male genitalia, be firm but gentle. The last thing you want to do is spoil your fun for life.

Gag him. When he cannot utter his protests, he may become more docile. Gagging is a sensitive activity – some people cannot bear it even for a second – but can be effective. If your slave has a gagging phobia, you may threaten him with it, but never actually do it. During gagging, three stomps on the floor, or another gesture, should replace the safeword. And never gag both nose and mouth at once, or when your submissive has a head cold.

The best gag is a pair of your own panties, preferably worn for at least one day, artistically stuffed into his mouth. Stockings or pantyhose are also useful. These soft gags are good for short-term gagging. Do not stuff them so far back in his mouth that he can't dislodge them if he needs to, and do not tie anything over them; if they work their way to the back of his throat, they could kill him.

Hard gags consist of a mouthpiece, usually made of plastic, and a strap around the head to hold the mouthpiece in. (Think braces and orthodontic appliances.) They include ball gags, penis gags (in which the submissive's mouth is clamped over a fairly realistic, if short, plastic penis), bits, and other toys available through mail order and in local sex shops. The ball gag is simplest; indeed, self-explanatory. The penis gag is especially humiliating to a straight male. The bit looks like a horse's bit but is made for a male's mouth; you may employ this in pony games. Most gags cause the submissive to salivate, so gags should not be so big as to make it impossible for him to swallow and/or to allow the drool to run out of his mouth.

Sensory deprivation. By controlling what your sub sees, hears, and smells, you can control him. The original idea of corner time or sending a misbehaving child to his room was to deprive him of social contact and limit the stimulation he could get, so he might calm down and reconsider his naughty behavior. Sensory deprivation in its various forms still works to punish the naughty and tame the defiant. Using several methods together is especially effective.

The simple blindfold may consist of a sleeper's black mask, a silk scarf or tie, panties bound on with stockings, or even a leather hood (of which more anon). Make sure he cannot see through, over, or under the blindfold. Once blindfolded, the submissive male may imagine dreadful chastisements approaching him, or even believe several Mistresses are in the room, all ready to humiliate and punish him. You may choose to tell him all about the coming punishment, or stay still and let him believe you have gone away. Unable to see, he is peculiarly vulnerable to fears of abandonment, cruelty, and public humiliation. Blindfolding is most useful in connection with various forms of bondage.

To prevent the sharp-eared slave from hearing you approach, you may fit him out with heavy ear protectors. Designed to prevent hearing loss when using noisy machinery, they are available in home centers and hardware stores, and, if your submissive ever uses power tools, you should have a pair anyway. Otherwise, good quality stereo headphones may serve as a substitute. The tiny portable type do not block sound at all.

The leather hoods always on display at sex shops may act as a combination gag, blindfold, and ear protector. Some Dommes find these hoods useful and attractive. By hiding the face completely, the hood provides total freedom and therefore total release. If you find them arousing, by all means enjoy them safely. I personally loathe them. By hiding the face completely, they prevent you from judging the effect of your words and actions on your willing submissive. But their use is entirely up to you.

Nipple Stimulation

Nipple stimulation deserves a section to itself because it is more than a form of coercion. It partakes of the nature of bondage (for it can be used as a form of restraint and may require various items of equipment) and of humiliation (for most males are secretly ashamed of having such a Feminine mark on their male flesh, and even more ashamed of deriving sexual pleasure from them). It is also intensely stimulating to many males, even those who have not yet discovered their submissive nature.

Hands, Teeth, and Household Items. The simplest, most sensitive instruments for nipple stimulation are your fingers. Pinch, tease, twist, and rub the nipples of a male, especially one in bondage, and watch him writhe in pleasure-pain. Use your fingernails to scrape and pinch as well. You may even nibble with lips or teeth.

The next step up is the improvised clamp made from a spring-type clothespin or the metal French clothespins found in camping stores and WalMarts everywhere. You may also experiment with hair clips of various types. Bobby pins may be slightly opened and then closed over the nipple. The viciously toothed clips used in salons to keep hair off your face may be too fierce for long use, but when rapidly opened and closed on the nipple create exquisite torment. You may even choose old clip earrings, especially those with screw-on posts, to decorate while stimulating.

Nipple Clamps and Weights. All sex-toy catalogues offer nipple clamps in a bewildering multitude of sizes and styles. Some snap on like the roach clips of old, while others screw on (and seem always to slip off). Some are toothed, others smooth. Some are joined with chains while others have hanging weights attached. And they range in price from reasonable to outrageous. All serve the same basic purpose.

Piercing. Permanent piercing of nipples, balls, cock, or wherever, should be done by a professional. Should you choose to pierce your submissive's nipples, go to a qualified piercer, make sure the instruments are absolutely sterile, and enjoy.

Play Piercing. If you have access to single-use sterile medical needles, you can do play piercing. Again, this (like fireplay, singletails, Japanese rope bondage, and so many of the other Leather arts) should be learned directly from a skilled Dom/me.

Bondage

Bondage may range from a firm but gentle tucking-in of the adult infant to the lengthy, savage captivity of a slave or votary undergoing an ordeal.

Bondage of any kind offers both comfort and unease. The comfort derives from the physical sensation of compression, which is soothing and pacifying, like being tightly held. The unease should be more psychological; it derives from the sensation of restraint, of being unable to get out, move freely, and exercise his will. Thus bondage is perfect, offering the Dominatrix free access to work her will upon her helpless captive, while producing in the slave the peculiar combination of stimulation and restraint that makes submission so satisfying for a naughty male.

First, a few warnings. Never leave a slave alone while he is in bondage. Never suspend anyone by the neck, or in such a position that his weight is borne by the neck. Make sure you can instantly release your submissive (keep a pair of heavy paramedic shears or tin snips nearby to cut the bonds, if necessary). And, if he begins to panic or uses the safeword, let him out immediately!

Standard Bondage Equipment. The choice of appropriate bondage equipment is a delicate one. Since it may also entail considerable expense, you should think through your fantasy (not to mention your slave's) before spending $359 on nonreturnable equipment you'll never use.

Submissives with Amazon or Goddess fantasies often prefer the studded black-leather gear widely available. It has an appropriately sinister, remote, and stylish feel, and it comes in an astonishing array of choices. However, the three domestic fantasies – the Nursemaid, Governess, and Queen fantasies – really demand a different type of equipment. Ropes, straps, and dog collars are more appropriate and erotic for them. Even in fantasy, nobody handcuffs a baby.

Almost everyone enjoys what I have called Victorian bondage: hobbles, corsets, and the backboard; these are discussed in a later section.

Adult infants need the simplest bondage, if any: tight sheets holding them tucked in bed; perhaps a strap to hold them down to a "changing table" while they undergo an enema or have their diapers changed. An adult schoolboy might need to be strapped down hand and foot to receive a particularly severe punishment. The sissy maid could lean either way, depending on individual taste. He may require more extensive bondage, even dungeon-type bondage, but he may not be attracted by the black-and-silver glitter of traditional gear.

Soft Bondage: Scarves and Neckties. Most bondage enthusiasts begin with soft bondage, tying up the submissive with scarves or neckties. This method seems comfortable and simple and has the advantage of being inexpensive, as long as you already own a brass bed or wooden four-poster. Yet the technique has certain disadvantages beyond the obvious one of permanently creased silk scarves. Depending on the cloth used, knots may slip out entirely, cutting off the scene, or tighten unexpectedly, cutting off his circulation. Knotting may be slow and awkward, and unknotting can be next to impossible. Do you really wish to cut your favorite scarf off your slave's ankles?

Choosing and Using Ropes. Soft all-cotton ropes may be used. (Nylon rope tends to slip.) An old, well-used clothesline may be ideal. If you desire, you may pad the ropes with soft cloth wound lightly around the joint to be tied. You will need to learn to tie some basic knots. Using the instructions in a camping guide or macrame handbook, practice until you can tie and untie the knots blindfolded. You must be quick and deft; few things are less erotic than a Mistress struggling with ropes while her bored and impatient submissive sighs with frustration.

Cuffs, Straps, Chains, and Belts. While you are learning the ropes, so to speak, you may use chains and/or buckled straps for bondage. Decent padded or fur-lined wrist and ankle cuffs are a basic necessity for the Domme's toybox. The studded black-leather type are widely available at sex shops, but for tiedowns and attachments you may prefer to buy dog or cat collars, which come in all colors, several widths, and a variety of lengths, from six inches to more than twenty. Some are too stiff to be used comfortably on human flesh, but others are slightly padded or lined with soft suede. Moreover, all have rings attached for leashes and are easily adjustable. They are rapidly attached and removed, and with a little simple modification, they can be locked. (Use one of the tiny locks sold as luggage locks; insert the shaft through one of the holes in the strap, enlarging it if necessary.) In short, they are ideal for a variety of bondage positions.

You may also use worn, soft leather or fabric belts when you need bonds with additional length. If either you or your submissive is handy with crafts, you may cut lengths of leather from a belt or a piece of leather to make lace-up manacles of precisely the right length. Use leather bootstrings for the laces, and finish with a small padlock.

Leashes of leather or metal are also useful gear. They may be fastened to a collar, to nipple clamps, to male chastity devices, or all three. They allow the Dominatrix to control her submissive while he is relatively mobile, and show off her power in a most humiliating fashion.

Collars. The collar to most Domestic Discipline practitioners is a useful place to attach a leash. In the Leather community, however, the collar is a symbol of commitment as powerful as a wedding band. Before you place a collar around a new sub's neck, make sure you know exactly what both of you mean by it. Many Leather people have collaring ceremonies to celebrate the commitment.

Collars themselves can range from a sissy's lace frill to an adult baby's bib, from a beautifully worked chain-and-leather waterfall to a short pearl choker indistinguishable from any other necklace except to those in the know. In some communities, only subs wear collars. However, the popular media often show Dommes in collars, so I've seen Dommes at parties wearing them. It's up to you and your sub to decide what each of you wears and what it means.

Spreader Bars and Dungeon Gear. Given the wide variety of available dungeon gear, you should be able to tie up your slave a new way every day, as long as you can afford the leather. Among the profusion of delightful instruments of restraint, a few old favorites stand out, always available and interesting. Steel handcuffs should be sturdy, professional-quality gear; cheap pairs often have nonstandard keys made of soft metal, and usually lack the ability to "double-lock" to prevent further tightening. Few people use handcuffs for lengthy bondage, as they can cut off circulation and cause nerve damage.

Spreader bars are designed to attach at the ankles and keep your submissive's legs apart so you can do whatever cock torture you please. Other dungeon gear includes (but is not limited to) wrist-to-thigh restraints, straitjackets, slings, and all the dozens of varieties of harness. Browse a catalogue together to choose these specialty items, which are too numerous to list here.

Victorian Bondage. Several types of restraint might appropriately be called Victorian bondage, because they derive directly from that fascinating moment in time. Corsets, hobbling, and the backboard all come under this heading, and, best of all, they may be used by a Mistress practicing virtually any fantasy.

- *The Corset.* Corsets may be associated with the Mistress, but are often worn by submissives as well. Their tightness, the erect posture they produce, and their Feminizing effect could make them suitable for a naughty schoolboy (sentenced to dress as a Female for teasing a little Girl, perhaps) and for a sissy maid. An Amazon or a Goddess might humiliate her slave by forcing him into the clothing of a Female, starting with the corset. Corsets are also widely available in dozens of styles. Choose carefully, and be willing to have one custom-fitted. Although they may be expensive, they are virtually indispensable for the submissive. Dommes, luckily enough, only have to wear them if they want to.

- *The Hobble.* Hobbling has, as yet, received too little attention in the literature. It derives from the hobble skirt of the 1870s (revived in the early years of the twentieth century), which was so narrow at the ankles that a Lady could barely toddle. By shortening the submissive's steps, the hobble makes him feel helpless and trapped; it eliminates any chance that he could run away. At the same time, it makes his gait and carriage more feminine, especially if he is also wearing corset and high heels. It may even impart a luscious Marilyn Monroe sway to his steps.

  The simplest hobble is still the hobble skirt, available from thrift shops or made at home. However, an excellent hobble can be improvised from a 12- to 14-inch chain (available by the foot at the hardware store) attached to leather ankle fetters. Never allow your submissive to climb stairs in a hobble.

- *The Backboard.* The backboard, too, is a truly Victorian accessory, historically used to correct the posture of generations of schoolGirls. It consisted of a padded wooden board with straps at shoulders and waist to hold the back rigidly erect and prevent the shoulders from drooping. The early Peter Weir film "Picnic at Hanging Rock" (besides being a good movie) has a backboard scene; you may wish to rent the film and examine the appliance.

  Unfortunately, I have never seen one offered in the catalogues, but if you and your submissive are handy, you may make one. Cut a piece of plywood to the length of your submissive's torso from shoulders to the tops of the thighs, slightly wider than the shoulders at the top and narrowing to the width of the hips. Pad it well with firm foam rubber and cover with a soft, absorbent material; velvet is best, but a good grade of terrycloth will do. Attach narrow vertical straps at the shoulders to hold the arm firmly to the backboard. Horizontal straps may run across the chest (just under the breasts) and at the waist and hips. You may indulge your imagination with decorations, ribbons, locks, and so forth, depending on whether you are training an adult infant to stand up straight or punishing a careless slave.

Bondage Positions

Many additional uses and techniques of bondage are given in the individual fantasy chapters, but the six basic positions are explained here. Whether your submissive is lying, standing, bending, sitting, kneeling, or walking, you can have the satisfaction of keeping him in bondage. Wonderful, isn't it?

Lying. The simplest bondage position is lying down, face-up, tied to a four-poster or a brass bed. In this position, with his legs spread and his arms immobile, you may Queen him, as explained later in this chapter; torment his nipples or his genitals; or indulge yourself with mockery at his helplessness. You may prop up his buttocks with pillows to gain better access to his anus and balls.

Standing. Ideally done in a doorway equipped with discreet eyebolts, this position presents you with many exciting possibilities. Hands overhead may be an uncomfortable position to maintain for long periods of time, but you may fasten his manacles to the eyebolts with enough slack so he can keep his circulation good. You can discipline him with paddle, crop, or birch; you may wish to tease his nipples, stimulate his anus, or mock him. A slave tied to the showerhead in a tub or shower may be disciplined or indulged with water sports. The Dominatrix may also tie her slave standing to a whipping post.

Bending. Combining standing and lying, this is absolutely the best position for discipline, as it presents the target area enticingly. The tightened skin even adds to the stimulation, making every blow more intense. You may tie your submissive over the arm of a chair or sofa, with his arms well stretched forward, or across a desk. Consider fastening the ankles as well to prevent kicking. You may also stimulate the anus in this position.

Sitting. A rare position, mostly useful for adult babies strapped into a feeding chair by means of a long strap around his waist and the seat.

Kneeling. Mostly useful for sissy maids and the slaves of Amazons and Goddesses. The ankles or knees could be fastened together. The wrists may be fastened behind the back or behind the back of the neck (a position that cannot generally be tolerated long). The Mistress may stand over the kneeling submissive for oral servitude, or force him to confess various fantasies and crimes.

Walking. Walking bondage may seem like a contradiction in terms, but it is actually very commonly used. A slave in a hobble and/or a corset may be free to walk and serve his Mistress, but he is also in bondage. One of the reasons for male chastity devices is to allow walking bondage. With a mobile yet bound vassal, the Mistress may enjoy all the privileges of being served, while maintaining a tight rein on her possession. The leash may be used to limit his freedom to a specific distance.

Male Chastity Devices

Like all bondage equipment, these range from the simple (straps and cock rings) to the elaborate (custom-made "permanent" chastity devices). The aim of all is to restrict the penis. Wearing some, the submissive may not even have an erection; others allow erection but make masturbation impossible. Still others are vibrating cock rings, designed to allow the Mistress total control of her slave's sensations and even his orgasm.

Who Should Use Them? Every Mistress, whatever her specialty, may find a use for these devices. It is just as important to keep Baby's mind pure and his flesh unpolluted as it is to control a wayward votary of the Goddess. Indeed, several of the more popular designs are based on Victorian originals, designed to prevent prisoners and children from the horrors of self-abuse.

Why Do They Work? All male chastity devices work on the basic principle that the Mistress who controls a male's penis controls him; not just his sexual satisfaction, but his thoughts, fantasies, will, actions, and emotions. The longer a vassal wears the badge of his servitude around his member, the more deeply submissive and obedient he will be. Therefore, the first treatment for a rebellious slave is affixing a chastity device to the root of his problems. The results are little short of miraculous: new gentleness, obedience, and humility in even the most recalcitrant males. Some few guysubs, however, do not respond well to this treatment. If chastity produces surliness or misery, choose another method for controlling him.

Chastity devices are not a panacea. They may help you gain command of an unruly male, but your own Authority must maintain that command. Furthermore, few chastity devices can be worn full-time. Most are designed to be worn for not more than an hour or so, especially if your submissive is well-endowed.

If chastity is a serious interest of yours, there are now some wonderful chastity devices that can be worn for months at a time. All are custom-made, and some are quite expensive, but luxuries make excellent holiday and birthday gifts. The Remy chastity is, in my experience, the best compromise for long-term wear without spending a fortune. However, it works best on submissives whose testicles are substantial in size. Access Denied, Northbound Leather, and various other makers have created luscious devices for short- or long-term wear.

Stiff Devices. Stiff devices are designed to be worn with a full or partial erection. They include most cock rings, ball stretchers, and harnesses. Stiff restraining devices intensify and contain the submissive's arousal. They prolong and control his erection, simultaneously tantalizing him while making any orgasm difficult, if not impossible. The longer any male is aroused, the more explosive will be his final orgasm; penis restraints not only make a male feel more submissive, they add to his pleasure when he is finally released. Many come fitted with locks, D-rings for leashes, and other security features to ensure that the naughty submissive may not remove the device himself. Few can be worn for longer than an hour. Custom-made chastities, however, may be worn for months.

Soft Devices. Soft devices are designed to prevent any erection. They generally consist of soft leather fitted to the hanging dimensions of the male (measuring him for the device is especially erotic and humiliating) or of metal strips arranged in a cage for the penis. Like stiff devices, they often feature D-rings and locking straps. The soft chastity device offers total control to the Mistress, for when a male loses his ability even to stiffen under stimulation, his spirit is halfway to being broken.

The one potential problem is that they must be fastened on when the submissive's member is in a flaccid state – hardly an easy task, as many males engorge as soon as they see the device. You may wish to force your submissive into a position of unusual pain, embarrassment, or humiliation (scrubbing toilets, for example) in order to fasten the device on him. Once attached, the device may be worn for many hours.

Vibrating Devices. The vibrating battery-powered cock ring controls the male in a somewhat different way. It ensures that he will have an orgasm on your command and at your will, without either of you actually touching the active member! By removing his control over the last personal power he has, that of orgasm, you gain total command of the submissive. Suggestions for use are given in the section on Combining Power and Pleasure, below.

CBT and Penis Punishment

From chastity devices the natural next step is CBT (cock and ball torture), also known as penis punishment. Few Nursemaids or Governesses will employ these techniques, but they are staples in the repertoire of the Queen, Amazon, and Goddess. Although they must be used with extreme care, these techniques are often highly effective in controlling the defiant or naughty submissive. Because the punishment is so severe, the submissive should be firmly in bondage before you proceed.

Specific techniques vary, but some suggestions follow:

- *Use a small cat o' nine tails to whip the cock and balls, never using your full force.*

- *Scrape your fingernails up and down his shaft, glans, and testicles.*

- *Use tweezers to pluck out individual pubic hairs.*

- *Scrape a small sharp-spined curler over the glans and scrotum.*

- *Rub the bristles of a hairbrush over the cock and balls.*

- *Drip hot candle wax over the glans.* Never use sealing wax, beeswax or a metallic candle; they can cause serious burns.

Verbal Humiliation

Some males need to be called naughty boys or told in no uncertain terms that they are wicked, worthless, or unmanly. Verbal humiliation, however, consists of more than just teasing. It is as delicate an art as proper birching and even more difficult to master. Before you try a scene including humiliation, talk it over with your submissive! If you inadvertently bruise his bottom, he will probably forgive you; if you mock his most sensitive point, you could wreck your relationship.

Verbal humiliation is most often talked of as a series of crudely expressed insults, generally aimed at the submissive's manhood and self-esteem. Some Mistresses practice this coarse form of a very fine art, mainly because some few males desire it. However, verbal humiliation can be a field of great creative potential. It may include the scolding of adult infants and schoolboys and icy directions to a sissy maid, as well as the straightforward and robust insults already mentioned. Furthermore, it can include forced confessions, interrogations, and whispered comments on the submissive's need for punishment and even Feminization.

The Enema

Many Dommes will at some time or other decide to cleanse the bowels of their submissives. Proper, careful techniques for enema administration are necessary; too much water or the wrong ingredients can lead to severe consequences, including a burst colon or death. Enemas should be used rarely, as they can interfere with natural bowel function. Despite these warnings, an enema can be a very erotic experience for a submissive and his Mistress. It is worth a careful try.

Equipment and Ingredients. Don't bother with chemical enemas of the Fleet type; the pleasure of the enema comes from the fullness of the bowel and the anal stimulation, not from cramping and elimination. Get a good rubber enema bag from a medical supply shop; it should have a rubber hose with clips to control the flow of water into the colon. The Bardex tip is inflatable so it won't pull out. Follow package instructions to the letter on sterilization and cleanliness!

Fill the bag with warm, not boiling, water; cold water should be avoided, as it causes cramps. No harsh detergents, no weird ingredients. Never use drugs or alcohol; they can lead to bleeding and even death from poisoning. The colon is a mucous membrane and as such absorbs chemicals far more readily than skin. Trust me, a pint to a quart of plain warm water will provide a very satisfying sense of fullness. The shame and drama you evoke are more likely to obtain good results than the most exotic ingredients imaginable.

Administration. Grease the nozzle with a lubricant and insert into the submissive's rectum. He should be lying on his side, knees drawn up. Let the water enter slowly, letting him grow used to the feeling of fullness. You may wish to set a kitchen timer and tell him he must hold in the enema until it rings in fifteen minutes. During the time he is holding in the enema, you may indulge in various other punishments and techniques, from scolding to bondage to a light spanking. (You may wish to paddle his hind end before the enema is administered, depending on your scenario.) You may also insert a butt plug to help him retain the water.

When it is time for him to relieve himself, most Mistresses allow the submissive to do so alone and in privacy. (You should discuss this issue with him before the scene.)

Afterward, you may make him stand in the corner, insert a vibrator in his anus, or go on with the scene in whatever way takes your fancy.

Anal Play

The voluptuous sense of being filled that penetration gives is not simply a female prerogative. (Though the passionate engulfing power of a pussy seizing and swallowing a cock is entirely ours.) You can thrill yourself and your submissive by slowly, inexorably penetrating his sweet rosebud anus.

Many men enjoy anal penetration; it stimulates the prostate and can be intense enough to cause orgasm with no direct touching of the cock. (This is a lot of fun for a Domme. Making him come - and come hard – without touching his cock is a genuine power thrill.) However, anal play requires gentleness, skill, and care to be safe and enjoyable. Keep your hands clean, and make sure you never transfer fluids, germs, your fingers, or other toys directly from anus to vagina. You can cause nasty infections that way. If you dislike mess or have cuts on your hands, wear rubber gloves and/or put down a towel.

A good manicure with short nails and smooth cuticles is essential. If you really want dragon-lady nails, don't penetrate your sub with your fingers. I usually have long nails on my left hand (perfect for CBT) and clipped nails on my right for penetration. Think of it as a Dommely fashion statement.

Although most people can do anal play without incurring serious medical consequences, a few people cannot, and you as the Domme are responsible for making sure that your sub is safe. Certain medical conditions, such as high blood pressure, make anal penetration or enemas risky. Beta-blocker drugs and certain other blood pressure and cardiac medications are particularly dangerous in conjunction with anal play. If your submissive has a heart valve prosthesis, he should not participate in anal play without his physician's explicit permission. Obviously if you want to practice anal stimulation, talk to your doctor.

If you're uncomfortable talking about this, maybe writing your doctor a note or asking over the phone would be wise – or getting a doctor you are comfortable with. In my experience, most doctors are much less shockable than patients think. But you should have a doctor whose judgment you trust and who is not judgmental about your sexual practices.

Once your doctor has cleared anal sex as safe, you need to assemble some toys and supplies. Lubricant is essential for any anal play. Despite Marlon Brando, butter is not an ideal anal lube. Dozens of brands of lube are available at your local drugstore or kink-store, but the choice depends on several factors. For anal play, nonoxynol-9 can be irritating to some people. Silicone-based lubes are wonderfully slick for finger-based penetration but will damage silicone toys. Many people find KY Jelly too light for anal play. My personal favorite is silicone-based, because I protect all toys, including the expensive and wonderfully jiggly silicone ones, with Saran Wrap or a condom to make cleanup easier.

Then there are the toys. Beads, butt plugs, dildos, vibrators, strap-on dildos, Tampax, your own hand... the variety is endless and wonderful, in size, shape, and material. Jellies are to my mind more fun than hard plastic vibrators. To me the silicone dildos are best of all, since they feel almost like real flesh. Anything you insert into the anus should have a flange at the bottom large enough to prevent its being sucked all the way in, or a string or other device to facilitate its removal.

Toys range in size from fingerlike to gargantuan. If you want to do a little fear play, make a sub look at a huge butt plug and then insert a smaller one. But all anal penetration should be done gently and in stages. Tearing anal tissues can cause scarring and eventual incontinence – a messy problem. Start small. You can always work your way up to the Giant Economy Vibe later. Remember that length and girth both matter.

Go step by step, slowly and gently. This is a process that should be savored. Don't start out penetrating with a twelve-inch strap-on as thick as a beer can. The first toy to use should probably be your finger. For mobility, length, and ease, the thumb is the best finger to start with. Make sure you use lots of lube, and let your partner get used to penetration over a course of weeks. Also, frankly, the possible negative results of rushing may include wrecking your chances – and your partner's! – ever to enjoy anal sex.

Make sure your partner gets lots and lots of pleasure. Stroke, hold, and stimulate him. You can try applying a vibrator to the base of a small butt plug buried in his ass or slipping on a vibrating cock ring to intensify the experience. Tease him by repeatedly penetrating him with a well-lubed thumb, moving shallowly at first and then easing in deeper. If it hurts, slow down and pull out a little. Relax, have a good time, and let the tension and excitement build. The more positive experiences your partner has with anal stimulation, the more eager he'll be for that full, final penetration.

Hair Removal

From the time of puberty, hair is a symbol of adulthood and sexual power. Removing your slave's pubic hair (or other body hair) shows not only that you own him but also that he is less than an adult. You may shave (using lots of lather), use bikini wax, pluck, or use chemical hair removers to denude your submissive of the hair on his chest, legs, buttocks, or armpits, and use any of these except chemical removal on his balls. And yes, the removal itself should be a shared erotic experience.

Hot wax is painful; be careful to purchase a type approved for the bikini area. Shaving is erotic but potentially dangerous; a nick is not unlikely. Yet soaping his balls for a shave is a thrilling sensation not to be missed. You may blindfold and tie your submissive during any of the techniques; he might jump less that way.

Face Slapping

Parents who slap their children's faces are doing something so dangerous that many highly trained, sadistic Leather people refuse to do it. Unprotected face-slapping can cause all kinds of problems, from detached retina to permanent hearing damage to whiplash. Yet face-slapping can be erotic; it is intensely powerful because of its emotional connotations.

To slap your sub safely, first make sure he is not wearing contact lenses. Then cradle his cheek in one hand, gently but firmly, while you tap or slap him lightly with the other, using the fingers, not the palm. This cushions the shock and prepares him for the blow; it can also become erotic in itself, since it demonstrates both tender care and urgent control.

Combining Power and Pleasure

How can you maintain command while you yourself are caught up in the throes of ecstasy? It may not be easy, but it is possible – and exceedingly rewarding to boot. Oral servitude, anal or vaginal, is the method of choice. But how exactly can you maintain your control over your slave while he is going down on you? That can be a tricky issue, and I have several concrete suggestions.

1. *Always refer to Cunnilingus in terms that you select.* Rendering obeisance, worshipping at your Shrine, oral servitude: these names all emphasize your Dominance and his low, groveling position. Remember the power of words. You may choose another name for the act, if you wish, but make sure it has the right connotations.

2. *Consider your position.* The classic posture, in which you lie on your back while the male serves you, may make him feel arrogant and in charge. Try Queening him. Have him lie on his back while you sit on his face (make sure he has an airway through either his mouth or his nose). It may take some time before you learn to have an orgasm this way, but it's worth the trouble.

    If you sit facing his body instead of his head, you can also engage in penis punishment, nipple pinching, and other delightful pastimes while he is serving you. Since the slave should be utterly forbidden to come (or perhaps even to become aroused) during the act of oral servitude, you can feel the proud sense of duty done whenever you tease and torment the submissive worshipping at your Shrine. Few things in a slave's or Mistress's life are as satisfying as this combined reward and punishment.

3. *Remind him of his subservience.* While he is rendering obeisance to your Shrine, talk to him. You may use verbal humiliation or simply tell him a fantasy demonstrating your total power and control. This approach is ideal for many Female Tyrants, who revel in the chance to speak harshly to their subordinates. However, for some Mistresses this technique works well only in the earlier stages of the service; they find it difficult to maintain a fluent conversation while approaching orgasm.

4. *Control his every move.* If you are lying on your back, take hold of a lock of his hair. Pull on it to bring him closer and intensify the feeling, pull him away from your Shrine to make him lighten up. (You certainly don't want to come too fast.) You can give him oral commands as well, indicating whether he is to go faster or slower, softer or harder.

    You may also forbid him certain acts, such as using his tongue, but if you do, you have to monitor him every minute, and be prepared to punish him instantly and memorably for any transgression. A riding crop applied to his back or buttocks is useful to indicate your displeasure.

5.   *Try remote control.* A vibrating cock ring with a variable-speed control is ideal for this task. You hold onto the control, turning up the intensity of the buzz when you are pleased with him, lowering it when you are displeased (or vice versa; just make sure he knows which is the reward and which the punishment!). Absolutely forbid him to have an orgasm, and make sure he understands the penalties of doing so without your express command. Then you can relax and enjoy a series of climaxes without worrying about losing the initiative.

Male chastity devices by their very nature keep him in check; somehow, when a man cannot attain or use an erection, he becomes a softer, humbler, more submissive creature. As stimulating as oral servitude is to the average submissive, he cannot express his arousal in any usual male-dominated way when his organ is bound. Instead, he must channel all the energy of his desire into the need to obey you. Stimulation plus frustration equals service.

These suggestions also work well for controlling your slave during anilingus, foot worship, massage, or any other personal pleasuring you choose. You should be able to attain climaxes of an extraordinary intensity and frequency, since the male cannot stop unless you order him to. Later on, his own orgasm (should you permit him one) will be intensified not only by the punishment, but also by the prolonged stimulation without release you have so kindly afforded him. If he isn't grateful, birch the little whelp.

Part Three

THE FIVE ARCHETYPAL FANTASIES

9

FANTASIES:
Discovering His, Fulfilling Yours

"To know is nothing at all; to imagine is everything." – Anatole France

The rich profusion of Female Domination fantasies may bewilder you at first. Possibilities abound: you may be a sophisticated siren luring a young man into your trap, a gracious lady accepting the homage of a knight, or a saucy Southern belle teasing her lover. Clearly these are different fantasies, demanding different approaches.

Clearly? Perhaps not. Diverse as they seem, all of these roles could fit into the same basic framework of fantasy, just as different pictures of the same size will fit into the same frame. However, by changing emphasis, interpretation, and script, they could also express totally dissimilar fantasies – or, if you will, fit into different frames.

This chapter simplifies choosing among the infinite variety of fantasies by classifying them into five archetypes, from the affectionate yet punitive Nursemaid to the stern and remote Goddess. As a matter of good form and relative importance, the fantasies are named after the Dominatrix in charge, even though the submissive in each fantasy has a different role: infant, schoolboy, sissy maid, slave, and votary.

Certainly a fantasy may partake of several of the archetypes; a Mistress may enjoy first the service due the Queen and then the adoration that delights the Goddess. Likewise, a submissive male may yearn to be caned like a naughty schoolboy, then sentenced to an hour or two of babyhood as additional humiliation. Nevertheless, you will find that the basic categories are useful, for they are based on genuine and enduring distinctions. The ritual exchange of power is the heart of any Female Domination fantasy, and in each archetype power has a characteristic source, balance, use, expression, and significance between Mistress and submissive. Furthermore, emotional distance (an indirect indicator of power) is different in each archetype.

Choosing a Fantasy

In one sense, even the most powerful Mistress does not choose a fantasy. Fantasies choose us. They appeal to us on a series of levels, from the deeply unconscious (in which the fantasy is a ritual reenactment or negation of an incident we cannot even remember – perhaps even from a past life), to the transparently superficial (liking the costumes).

As you read the next five chapters, you should have no trouble at all telling which roles you would like to try out. The jolt of sexual electricity should immediately tell you. You may even be tempted to quit reading. Why grope around for something else when you've found exactly what you've always wanted?

Because something else may be even more fun for you than your first pick. Because your partner may respond better to a different version of the Dominance/submission scenario. Because variety is the spice of life.

Quit reading, if you like, and go tie up your submissive. But when the scene is over, go back and read the parts you skipped. You may find an idea, a technique, or a scenario that instantly rouses all your Dominant instincts.

You could recognize elements of your submissive's fantasies in another archetype, giving you a new and delightful way to surprise him. Most submissives are touchingly grateful when a Mistress puts a new spin on an old scene. Besides, why should your vassal always have to come up with new ideas for his Domination?

Or you could, weeks or months from now, find yourself toying with an idea picked up from a different fantasy. Perhaps, while playing out your basic fantasy, you could adapt a technique from a totally different archetype of Female Dominance. An Amazon might humble her slave by making him write punishment lines as a Governess would, then revert to type and shackle him to the bed so she could use him sexually. A Queen could shame her sissy maid by putting him into diapers as a Nursemaid would. Or the gentle Nursemaid might adapt the Amazon's wicked interrogation technique in order to find out what naughty little boy stole a cookie from the cookie jar.

The possibilities are endless. Don't limit your options by defining yourself too narrowly. You may be a Goddess or a Nursemaid, but first and foremost you are a Woman in charge. If you try a new technique and find it disappointing, or your submissive doesn't care for it, no harm has been done. Next time try something else.

The Five Fantasies

The five basic archetypes of Female Dominance are briefly explained below. The accompanying table summarizes all this information and gives additional considerations; you may wish to study it before turning to the individual chapters. You may read your favorite first and then browse through the others at your leisure. Rereading can be helpful; an idea might strike you on the third reading that you missed entirely the first and second times.

Although most fantasies fall into one of the categories, the classification is neither rigid nor mutually exclusive. Most Dominant Women also freely borrow techniques, attitudes, dialogue, and costumes from other categories. Nevertheless, the archetypes are helpful, because they express very real differences in the use and distribution of power, in the types of Dominance and submission they entail, and in the attitude to pain. Like colors, they are instantly identifiable in their pure forms, but they also take a thousand other forms by blending one with another.

The Nursemaid. The most affectionate of all the Mistresses, the Nursemaid has charge of a submissive who pretends to be a naughty but adorable baby ranging in age from newborn to four or five years old. Sometimes the adult infant is identified as a Female baby, expressing his sense of his own helpless sweetness and need for nurture. The Nursemaid coddles, cuddles, and disciplines the child, occasionally also attending to his health needs by administering an enema. The pleasure for the submissive lies in lots of attention and total freedom from responsibility. The pleasure for the Dominant lies in her absolute power and in the sheer fun of playing with a baby.

The Governess. The Governess is unrelentingly stern. She teaches and disciplines a submissive whose fantasy age may range from schoolboy to college age. Of all fantasies, this one is probably least explicable to those who do not share its hypnotic charms. The arousal and the release are not provided by cuddling (as in the Nursemaid fantasy) or by more adult forms of sexual contact (as is often the case in the three following archetypes), but by the process of anticipating and experiencing physical discipline. The focus of this fantasy is almost pure punishment; there is rarely any sexual contact (unless the boy has been caught masturbating). The submissive takes his pleasure in the punishment itself and the subsequent release from guilt. The Mistress enjoys her power of inflicting the punishment and her sense of her own moral superiority.

The Queen. This fantasy allows both partners to feel pampered and special. The Queen, served hand and foot by her sissy maid, enjoys having the housework done, her personal desires fulfilled, and every command obeyed. She may be a stern employer, a wicked secretary who turns the tables on her boss, or an aunt with advanced ideas on teaching young males respect for the Female sex. In whatever guise, she forces her submissive male to serve her and render obeisance to the Shrine of her Womanhood. She may also choose to punish him severely for any breach of decorum.

In token of his respect for Femaleness, the submissive also wears Feminine clothing, which may range from a hidden pair of sissy panties to full Feminization, up to and including padded bras and girdles, stockings, dresses, high heels, and wigs. This experience is both an honor (for, within this fantasy, the Female sex is superior) and a deep shame to him (for, within this fantasy, all males are unworthy to dress in such garb). The sissy maid, freed from the dull conformity of masculine attire and societal roles, luxuriates in the soft textures and tender colors of Female garb, while being voluptuously punished for his forbidden desires.

The Amazon. The relationship between Amazon and slave varies, depending on the scenario chosen. In some fantasies the two are almost equals; her advantage is that she has captured him and is preparing to test his mettle as a male by tormenting him in various imaginative ways. The slave may try to escape or rebel, but he is always recaptured and conquered by the Amazon's strength and intelligence. In other versions of the fantasy, the submissive is a totally crushed and obedient slave, tormented just for pleasure. In the first version, the submissive may actually dare to wrestle his Dominatrix. In either case, the slave's respect for his Mistress is not the childlike awe of the adult infant or schoolboy or the devoted worship of the sissy maid or the Goddess's votary. It is compelled by her physical Domination of him, and it includes both respect and desire. Thus the pleasure of this fantasy lies in the testing and proving of the Mistress's authority and the slave's submission, plus a healthy dose of sheer pleasure at inflicting – or receiving – pain.

The Goddess. The Goddess is one of the sweetest of all the Dominant roles a Woman may assume, for the Goddess is served, worshipped, and obeyed simply because she is a superior Female. In this role, the Dominatrix may demand hours of oral servitude, foot massage, and other personal services, and reward them with perhaps a remote smile or a new type of penis punishment.

Her votary or slave often suffers punishment for various transgressions. He may also be forced to undergo ritual torments, designed to prove his devotion, but he is also willing to rub, stroke, lick, massage, and otherwise demonstrate his adoration and respect for his Lady's sacred flesh. The Goddess is, of course, immeasurably distant from her votary, and he is touchingly grateful for any mark of her notice, even if it would (under ordinary circumstances) be a humiliation rather than a reward."

Fantasies In Conflict

Your own preferences are your best guide to what you should try next, along with any suggestions by your submissive that you care to heed. But what if your fantasies are very different?

Mistress Kay, a Dominatrix of my acquaintance, is a natural Amazon, eager to overcome her slave's rebellion and test his manhood. Unfortunately, her submissive, Timmy, prefers the role of scared schoolboy, baring his naughty bottom for the paddle. Although his fantasy allows her to heap punishment on him – a process she enjoys – she would also like to extend his submission to more areas. An Amazon's slave usually has to undergo CBT and verbal humiliation, which Timmy doesn't care for.

Furthermore, an Amazon's slave is expected to rebel occasionally – even try to escape – so the Amazon can prove her power by placing him in bondage. Unfortunately, Timmy hasn't the spirit to rebel. His worst escapade occurred when he dared to stick out his tongue at Mistress Kay. Although she enjoyed washing out his mouth with soap and giving him a lengthy strapping, she later came to me, seeking advice.

"He isn't really interested in obeying me," she said angrily. "All he cares about is his stupid paddling. He tells me he wants to submit, but he always ends up controlling the situation. Sometimes I feel like giving up."

Knowing Timmy and Mistress Kay as well as I did, I realized that this problem, as upsetting as it was, could never destroy their relationship. They were very deeply committed to one another. However, in similar situations, some couples have been unable to work out a compromise and have subsequently broken up over the choice of fantasy. And it was clear that Kay was extremely upset. Something had to be done immediately.

I talked to Timmy alone to get his perspective on their problem. "Yeah, I know she wants to do all those weird things to me," he said. "But I'm a simple guy. I don't want to be tied up and teased with feathers. All I want is a good spanking and then to have her cuddle me. Why does she have to force this other stuff down my throat?"

After several lengthy discussions between Kay and Timmy, with advice and help from me and several other Mistresses, we came up with several solutions to the problem. Timmy could enjoy his schoolboy status half the time, playing out Kay's fantasy the rest of the time. He could combine his preferred games with some elements from hers, while still avoiding the CBT he dreaded. Or he could continue clinging to his schoolboy fantasy, knowing that Kay was playing out her Amazon fantasy with other, more pliable submissives.

Faced with these choices, Timmy realized how selfish he was being. He had been so caught up in the childish fantasy that he was acting like a child about the issue. He and Kay decided to compromise. He has grown to appreciate the pleasures of bondage and of rebellion, and Mistress Kay finds it more satisfying to punish him as he desires, knowing that she is going to get some satisfaction as well.

Hints on Resolving Conflicts

A great deal of the problem between Kay and Timmy was rooted in the fact that they never discussed they wanted sexually except during the fantasy sessions. Unfortunately, they were also so deeply embedded in their roles that they couldn't deal with each other as adults who needed consideration and respect. Kay was apt to be and sound dictatorial, tending to ride roughshod over Timmy's wants and needs. In turn, Timmy was whiny and uncooperative. Just like the child he was playing, he wanted what he wanted and he wanted it now!

When they talked over the problem away from the fantasy, Timmy was more able to see that Kay deserved to have the satisfaction of enacting her favorite scenarios. Likewise, Kay could understand that Timmy's resistance rose, not from any indifference to her feelings, but from defensiveness. He desperately needed the schoolboy scenario, and he was afraid that if he became an Amazon's slave instead of a schoolboy, he would never get what he needed.

So if you have a conflict over fantasy, wait a day or two to discuss it, and talk it over like adult, equal partners, not like a Dominatrix with her slave.

Sometimes it helps for each partner to write down his or her ideal fantasy, along with some reasons why it appeals. A submissive who loves the sheer sensual pleasure of serving a Queen would list that as a pleasure to him. If his Dominatrix wants to act out a Nursemaid fantasy, she could make sure that her baby was wrapped in the softest, most Feminine of baby clothes. A submissive who longs for the intense sensation and sense of overwhelming physical risk of dealing with an Amazon might have problems with a Mistress whose chief interest is in being a Queen. Yet, if she emphasizes the humiliation and the danger of dressing in female clothing, and indulges him with floggings every time he makes a minor slip in serving her, the two fantasies can work well together.

The key lies in identifying what each fantasy does for the two participants. Although I have provided a general guide to the pleasures of the fantasies, each individual will have a different reaction. Talk over what excites you about the fantasy. What else do you feel, along with pain and pleasure and power?

Often the subsidiary emotions are the most important. For example, Mistress Kay was aroused by the idea of quelling a rebellious slave; she felt mean just whipping a helpless schoolboy. When Timmy agreed to be a bit more defiant, both enjoyed the Governess sessions more. For his part, Timmy felt safe with the schoolboy fantasy, because he knew exactly how much punishment he would get. He felt too frightened at the idea of being in an Amazon's power to find it sexually stimulating. When Kay promised him not to go beyond his limits, and faithfully to release him if he used the safeword, he was more able to relax and enjoy the additional stimulations of being a captive.

Most fantasy conflicts can be resolved with a little compromise and some adult thinking. Share, talk, love, and reveal your hearts to one another. Don't fall into the trap of using the fantasy itself to punish each other. If a conflict comes up in the fantasy world, don't try to resolve it by longer or harder scenes. Discuss it as adults, as equals, as lovers, as friends. Not as Mistress and submissive. Using fantasy to avoid conflict only makes it worse in the end.

10

THE NURSEMAID:
Diaper Discipline and Other Nursery Tricks

"Heaven lies about us in our infancy! Shades of the prison-house begin to close upon the growing boy." – William Wordsworth, "Ode: Intimations of Immortality"

The Mistress who enacts the Nursemaid fantasy enjoys the intoxicating sensation of complete power over her submissive. Few submissive males are as readily dominated as the adult baby. Moreover, in this fantasy the Mistress and submissive are unusually close and intimate; the emotional distance so often part of Amazon and Goddess fantasies would be completely inappropriate here.

For the submissive, the Nursemaid fantasy is a trip back in time, to the cataclysmic era of infancy. No baby understands that things change, that what he is experiencing in this moment is not eternal. To an infant, all sensations are overwhelming: he is totally helpless, totally loved, totally punished.

The intensity of these feelings is enhanced by his absolute irresponsibility. A baby has no duties; he cannot serve, work, plan, or decide. All he can do is feel. He luxuriates in sensations, emotional and physical, piercing, tumultuous, ecstatic. Some of these delights are, understandably, forbidden to the adult: the warm wet pleasure of soggy diapers, for example, or the bliss of drinking from a nippled bottle. If modern society permitted such indulgences, no one would ever get any work done; we would all be occupied in counting our toes, sucking our thumbs, and keeping one hand down our diapers, exploring the various features of our hidden physiognomy. Also, there would be no one to change those diapers when they grew chilly and uncomfortable, to bring us bottles, or to tuck us in at night.

The Elements of Fantasy

The Nursemaid fantasy is designed to make the submissive feel loved and protected, on the one hand, and thoroughly embarrassed and punished, on the other. In short, to re-create infancy in all its aspects. A careful Mistress will see to it that the script, costumes, and setting all maintain the illusion of an all-powerful, punitive, yet loving Nursemaid in charge of a helpless, punished, yet secure baby.

The Script. A simple script is best for this fantasy. While enacting the role of an infant, your submissive is incapable of making lengthy confessions or performing complex service. You as Nursemaid will be making all the decisions, which is common among Female Domination fantasies, but also doing all the work, which is not always true of other fantasy roles. Indeed, the question of who is really in charge always intrudes on these scenarios. Although the baby ends up well-punished, he is also a tiny autocrat, demanding food, attention, care, and fussing from his devoted Nursemaid.

Specific script ideas include the classic Aunt, Nursemaid, and Babysitter scenes; they differ only in the relationship of the Dominant Female to the infant. This is one of the few fantasies in which a Mommy figure may take part; Mothers themselves are generally not erotic, though a powerful Mother figure is important to many Female Domination fantasies.

The submissive's fantasy age may range from newborn infant to three or four years old. Older children get into more trouble; younger ones require more loving attention.

Costumes. Your adult baby needs many of the costumes a chronological infant finds useful. First and foremost, he should have diapers. No baby is well-dressed without them. Large-sized diapers for incontinent adults are available in any drugstore; mail-order houses and Internet sites offer specialty items, such as rubber or plastic pants, cloth diapers, and adult-size baby clothing. Bibs, smocked dresses, lace caps, booties, and ankle socks may also be needed.

You may wear a nurse's white uniform, complete with white shoes and stockings, or dress as a teenage babysitter or in other Women's clothing. For the Mommy of a young infant, a snap-open nursing bra is a nice touch. Exotic dress, heavy perfume, long scarlet nails, and startling makeup are as out of place here as they would be in any nursery. A sense of warm, clean, safe comfort is the goal.

Setting and Props. The nursery itself may be any bedroom, but one decorated for an infant, featuring lots of pink and blue ruffles, lambs and bunnies, and a softly shaded night light is best. The baby should have toys appropriate to his age and sex; stuffed animals are a favorite, along with rattles, pacifiers, and books of nursery rhymes for Mommy to read aloud. The only appropriate music is children's music, either recorded favorites or the Nursemaid's own lullabyes, sung in the twilight to put baby to sleep.

Of course, no nursery would be complete without a few baby bottles, pacifiers, baby powder, and a changing surface of some kind. A potty chair is also a nice touch for Nursemaids who have older charges or who give frequent enemas. Adult sizes are available from medical-supply houses; although they are forbiddingly utilitarian, they can be decorated in a nursery motif. A ruffled skirt is easy to add and won't interfere with emptying the pot itself. A small wooden chair for corner time, a wooden hairbrush to maintain discipline, and of course an enema kit are also necessary.

The Skills of a Nursemaid

What makes a Mistress a good Nursemaid? Genuine affection for your charge, no matter how troublesome he may be, is the first requirement. You may have to discipline his naughty bottom or teach him the value of good health with a clyster, but your firmness must be tempered by warmth and care. After all, you are doing this not for your own sake, but for his.

Diapers. If you have ever cared for a chronological infant, you will know exactly what the adult baby wants and needs. Wearing diapers is ungainly and shameful but warm and erotic for him as well. Having the diapers changed entails not just the removal of one garment and the substitution of another, but all the ritual of washing, drying, powdering, applying ointment, and so forth. This ritual can be the focus of a great deal of erotic play. It is, in fact, the usual way for the submissive to achieve orgasm.

Spankings and Corner Time. Nevertheless, you must maintain a strong Authority. When your submissive throws a tantrum, disobeys your diaper rules, or otherwise displeases you, you must be prepared to intervene drastically. The classic punishment for such naughty behavior is a sound spanking, in the classic over-the-knee position, using your hand or a hairbrush. Caning, strapping, and birching are not to be thought of: too severe for baby's tender skin.

The question of whether to leave diapers on or take them off is frequently debated. Although a bare-bottom spanking is classic, a soiled diaper is definitely best left on, no matter what tradition says. A wet diaper might be spanked dry, or the soggy diaper could be pulled down to expose the damp skin, which increases the sting.

The intensity of an adult infant's spanking should vary with the situation. Ordinary naughtiness may demand a brief flurry of fairly hard spanks, but a longer spanking should start slow and build in weight and intensity. (The greater the submissive's excitement, the more pain he can take.) Confine the smacks to the plump lower portions of the nether cheeks, always remembering that the sweet spot where a spanking tingles most delectably is in the center of the lower curve. If the submissive's bottom is cushioned by diapers, you may strike harder.

You may begin with several light stinging smacks, slapping the buttocks briskly to get the circulation going. Then add a little more force until the buttocks are rosy and the submissive is reacting with sobs or moans. Finish up with a few heavier, deeper blows, smacking well until the naughty submissive is thoroughly punished. He may stop wriggling, he may cry real tears (although this is relatively rare), but he will definitely stop resisting the smacks and become contrite.

After the spanking, you may make your naughty submissive stand in the corner, holding his skirts above his waist to display the well-spanked, reddened bottom. For some submissives, this position is more humiliating than the spanking itself, but it is only appropriate for an adult toddler or an older boy. (Babies don't stand.)

Enemas. The diaper seems to lead naturally to the enema (or clyster, a pleasantly old-fashioned word for the practice). Details of safe, erotic enema administration were given in Chapter 8, but the Queen's enema (sounds like a bad historical novel) or the purge an Amazon gives her slave is very different in tone and style from the warm, affectionate nursery clyster.

To make the enema a pleasurable experience, you should decide whether the procedure is a punishment or a health measure and script the scene accordingly. If it's a punishment, what was your submissive's crime? Commonly, clysters are mandated to cure the naughty one of wetting or soiling his diapers; to cleanse him of disobedient thoughts or actions (a clean mind in a healthy body); to cure temper tantrums; to aid in toilet training; to prevent or punish masturbation; to soothe fretfulness and colic. All of these reasons serve either the health or the punishment scenarios, but your script will differ, depending on which you choose.

The health enema should be surrounded by evidence of your solicitous concern for his well-being. Fuss over him, telling him how much good the enema will do him, how strong and healthy he will be when he has been thoroughly purged. Never remind him that it will help him grow up to be a big boy. That's the last thing he wants. Praise him for taking lots of fluid (no matter how little you are actually giving him) and promise him treats and candy for being so brave.

The punishment enema should be given in an atmosphere of mixed sorrow and anger. Instead of praise and solicitude, offer a sad little lecture on how sorry Nursey is that she has to do this, how the fluid will swell him up and make his tummy hurt, and what dire consequences will result if he should let even the tiniest drop leak from his naughty bottom. While the submissive is holding in the fluid, you may emphasize his punishment by giving him a mild to moderate spanking. The pain of the spanking, added to the unaccustomed fullness in his churning bowels and his frantic desire not to disgrace himself with an accident, may be the ultimate thrill for an adult infant.

If you have a potty chair, now is the time to seat him in it. If he persistently holds onto the enema, threaten him with a spanking, whether it was ostensibly given for punishment or health reasons. Praise and fuss over him once he has emptied his bowels, telling him that now he'll be a good (or healthy) little baby. You might even wash him up, though a few Mistresses prefer to let baby wipe himself.

The Pleasures of a Nursemaid

Singing, cuddling, playing nursery games can be a warm, affectionate, and intimate way of spending time with your submissive. The Nursemaid enjoys the gentleness of her fantasy scenario and the sensual pleasure of touching a man anywhere she desires – with no taboos, no sexual demands, just power, pleasure, cuddling. Furthermore, the enemas and diapering provide her with a sense of intimacy as well as the secret joy of playing with forbidden substances. By totally accepting her submissive's helplessness, his bodily wastes, his tears, his need for consolation and discipline, the Nursemaid gives him what he needs – and herself all the power and satisfaction of mothering.

The Needs of a Baby

The needs of an adult baby are not difficult to understand. He doesn't yearn to suffer through ordeals to prove his manhood. He wants to forget his manhood (with all its associated macho posturing, cut-throat competition, lies and insincerity, and adult worries) and return to the simplicity, warmth, and attention he had (or needed) in his earliest years. If you can offer him affection, attention, and some discipline, he will reward you with pleasant play and great affection.

Enacting the Scene

Act One: Establishing Your Authority. The adult baby is unlikely to challenge your authority per se, although he may throw an occasional tantrum. Nevertheless, this stage is crucial in the Nursemaid fantasy, not as a test of your Rule, but as a distinctly pleasurable experience in itself. During this time, you may choose to indulge yourself and your submissive in any combination of the following activities:

- *Dressing him in baby clothes*
- *Diapering (these first two are de rigueur)*
- *Playing with infant toys*
- *Playing peekaboo and other baby games*
- *Putting him down for a nap*
- *Telling bedtime stories*
- *Cuddling*
- *Using a pacifier*
- *Bottle feeding*
- *Feeding him baby food*
- *Nursing him at the breast*
- *Tying him to the crib so he won't fall or crawl out*
- *Toilet training*

Act Two: Transgression and Punishment. Sadly, even in the cozy paradise of the nursery, crime and punishment must obtrude. An adult baby may throw a tantrum, necessitating a spanking, or he may wet or soil his diapers, making the administration of an enema a desirable punishment. You may also choose to sentence your submissive to corner time, stammered apologies, or perhaps slapped fingers.

Begin the punishment with a scolding. Pull the miscreant over your lap and pull up his skirts, exposing the diaper. Depending on your mood and the condition of the diaper, you may wish to begin the castigation with the diaper still covering his rosy bottom, later progressing to a bare-bottom spanking. With the naughty baby over your lap, lecture him sternly, but in terms he can understand, telling him how disappointed Mommy [Auntie, Nursey] is with his behavior. Though it saddens you to be forced to spoil his day with a spanking, it would be far worse to spoil him for life by not correcting his infant wickedness. Similar techniques are useful in the administration of the clyster.

The adult baby is usually happy to break down in sobs (not tears) at the threat of losing Nursey's love. He will be contrite and sweet after punishment, hoping to win back his Mistress's lost love.

Act Three: Consolation. Consolation for the adult infant is strikingly similar to the establishment of your authority. It may consist of cuddling, games, kisses, and so forth. However, to bring the game to a close, you should detect baby's need for a new diaper. While changing him, you may surreptitiously rub and fondle him, until he wets the diaper in a somewhat more adult manner.

Variations on the Fantasy

You may choose to use the Nursemaid fantasy as an adjunct to a Governess or even Queen fantasy. In that case, the Nursemaid emerges as a punishment for some crime in the other fantasy. A naughty young boy might well be punished for disobedience by a temporary relegation to nursery status. A sissy maid who is slovenly in his work or dress might be punished by taking away the maid's uniform, diapering until he wets himself, and (to make sure no more untoward accidents occur) the thorough internal cleansing of an enema. During the time that you are conducting the fantasy, you must treat your submissive as an infant. He cannot be expected to recite lessons or provide maid service now.

11

THE GOVERNESS:
The Power of Discipline

"Management has announced that beatings will continue until morale improves." – sign on office wall

The Governess is the purest of the archetypal fantasies. Its success is not dependent on elaborate scripts, fine costumes, or other paraphernalia. To be a good Governess, you must maintain authority and supply chastisement. That's it.

The charms of this fantasy are almost unexplainable to anyone not a devotee. "Why would anyone want to be spanked?" ask many confused potential Mistresses. "Doesn't it hurt?"

Yes, it hurts. But many people – not all of them submissive males – find the anticipation, performance, and aftermath of chastisement to be intensely erotic. The usual explanation is that rituals of spanking recall childhood punishments that accidentally roused the first fires of sexuality. However, many spanking lovers were never so punished in their youth. Yet something has created a voluptuous fascination with the details of punishment. It may be genetic; many devotees say they've been enthralled with spanking as long as they can remember.

And this is a very common fantasy, one of the most common. Plenty of Hollywood movies, romance novels, and old comic strips mention this practice (although often with a Female in the position of indignity). Clearly the subject of spanking has a sexual dimension for many people, however little they wish to admit it.

For submissive males, there are plenty of cultural references to keep them in a state of constant arousal: stories of the canings at British boarding schools, the judicial floggings that took place even in our own country (the last one was in

Delaware in 1952!), and the Singapore caning of 1994, which demonstrated to many people that a swipe across the butt could indeed range from a gentle swat to a scarring experience.

Whatever causes this fetish, it is typically almost obsessive. Nobody ever manages to quit the fantasy for long, and most spankophiles say, despite the pleasures of vanilla sex, that nothing else provides the same intensity of feeling that a good long punishment session creates. So if you're in love with a submissive man who wants and needs Governess-style punishment, either resolve to supply it or consider getting out of the relationship.

The Elements of Fantasy

Minor variations in script, costumes, and setting may add spice to this fantasy, but the central drama is always the same. However, choosing the right implement can be vital. Read and study the detailed suggestions given in Chapter 7, making note of all the delicious variations. Then arm yourself with your chosen implement or implements, and enjoy!

The Script. The basic script is always the same: the schoolboy sins, suffers, and repents. Yet that structure need not limit your creativity in planning scripts. There are dozens of ways in which a naughty male might find himself at the mercy of an angry Female with vengeance on her mind and a paddle in her hand.

Costumes. Some of the classic schoolboy fantasies benefit from good costumes, especially the Nurse fantasies, which are a special favorite with many submissives. However, most Governess-style fantasies don't require much in the way of costuming for Dominatrix or submissive. On the other hand, most submissive males enjoy being disciplined by a Female wearing a skirt, a slip, or even a corset and stockings.

You may, if you wish, design a special punishment costume for your submissive male, consisting of a shamefully short baby-doll nightgown. Many schoolboys find Feminization of any kind extremely humiliating; they don't give it the honor and reverence typical of a sissy maid or a votary. You may wish to try it on your submissive.

Setting and Props. The setting may be a spare bedroom or any other room in your house. If your submissive enjoys a full-fledged schoolboy fantasy, a desk and chalkboard are desirable. You may wish to bend your naughty submissive over the arm of a sturdy couch or chair, across a table top, or over the end of a bed for his chastisement.

As for props, none are needed for most fantasies except the basic bondage gear and of course the necessary punishment equipment. Make sure you have a sturdy wooden hairbrush, a flexible leather strap, and a good paddle. Riding crops, birches, and cats are really luxuries, although agreeable ones. (The Governess fantasy is usually the least expensive to set up; the Queen is usually the most expensive, although you have to factor in the value of the maid service.)

The Skills of a Governess

The skills a Governess needs are covered in glowing detail in Chapter 7, where a multitude of exciting possibilities are presented for your entertainment and the education of your submissive. You should read and re-read that chapter, paying special attention to the types of blows and the signs that your submissive has been sufficiently punished.

But, since you will be doing a great deal of pounding of bare backsides, perhaps a warning is best placed here. Especially with the narrow, flexible implements – the cane, the riding crop, the switch, and the birch – you must be careful. Don't start out with full force. Though the blows may produce real reddening of the buttocks and even occasionally real tears, you don't want to make scars or open wounds. (Infection is always possible when blood flows.)

Instead of trying to produce submission with raw pain, use psychology. Your submissive wants and needs the total experience of a spanking, not just the blows on the buns. And the total experience includes fear, anticipation, tension, respect for the Female, and distress at having upset her. It may also include rebellion and defiance, which you must put down with a firm hand, unless he's using the safeword. (If he is, stop the scene immediately!)

Despite the simplicity of this fantasy, you can't get away with aiming half a dozen lackadaisical smacks (or even a dozen hard ones) at your slave's bottom, while saying in a bored voice, "Bad boy needs a spanking." Summon some energy and some creativity. Make him scared to lie over your lap but far more scared to defy you, and you'll have a good scene going.

Additional Penalties. Some schoolboys need additional penalties: punishment writings (think Bart Simpson, writing 100 times on the board), servitude, corner time, etc. These depend on the crime, the scenario, your desires, and your submissive's needs. Some schoolboys like to be Feminized after a serious spanking.

The Pleasure of a Governess

Administering a serious (or even a playful) chastisement can be as exhilarating as a fast walk on a crisp windy day. It combines all the physical pleasures of any good aerobic exercise with an intense, arcane eroticism – the naked bottom, bared and helpless; the cries and writhings of the submissive; the sense of power. To some extent, anything rhythmic reminds us of sex, and nakedness plus rhythmic force plus that indefinable satisfaction of the Dominatrix in control is an intensely erotic pleasure.

More than that, the Governess archetype is about administering pain, or painful pleasure. A Governess whose naughty schoolboy craves punishment has the satisfaction of giving him what he needs and wants, while feeding the secret darkness in her soul. Coming to terms with the joys of sadism-a word few spankophiles are comfortable with – is considerably easier when you have an ardent, eager submissive begging for the lash.

The Needs of a Schoolboy

The punishment the schoolboy craves is physically stimulating and emotionally cleansing. In submitting to the chastisement, whether it's a brief hand spanking or a lengthy, multi-implement extravaganza, he seeks not just the rhythmic blows and reddened bottom, but a mystical sense of losing his will, his identity, and his sins in a gigantic emotional abyss.

The pain, suspense, and fear of a spanking carry him out of his ordinary life and into an almost druglike state. To reach that nirvana, he goes through a series of changing reactions: Excitement, physical pain, rebellion, submission, and ultimately peace. The following process may not hold true for every spanking devotee, but it seems to be accurate for most.

- *Excitement.* He feels this rising emotion, really a mingling of anxiety and sexual arousal, during the period of anticipation, when the submissive knows he will be spanked but the chastisement hasn't started yet.

  As the spanking grows closer and closer, anxiety may begin to replace the arousal, and he could try to get out of the spanking. Unless he uses the safeword, go ahead and spank him, no matter what he says he wants. He's trying to test your limits, but he would be disappointed if you didn't give him the whaling he needs.

  Try to extend this period as long as you can. The more aroused, excited, scared, and tense he is before the actual chastisement, the more intimidating it will seem. Since the emotional catharsis is what he needs, emotional tension is necessary to achieve it. (If this concept isn't clear to you, go back and reread the chapters on establishing and asserting your authority, as well as the invaluable advice in Chapter 7.)

  You may extend the time with scoldings, descriptions of the dreadful whipping to come, corner time, and various preparations of the seat of the action. You could tell him that the spanking will begin in precisely fifteen minutes, and make him stand in a corner, his pants around his ankles, watching the clock. The whole time he will be anticipating the first bite of the switch into his unprotected bottom, wondering whether he will be able to bear the pain, and alternating miserably between wishing the waiting was over and hoping that the time will never pass.

Don't forget to make him fetch the implement (or implements) of his correction and to make him beg you for chastisement. Then place him in position, binding him if necessary, and delay some more. Don't start the actual punishment until he's ready to beg you for a whipping, just to end the suspense.

- *Physical Pain.* Now that he's in a state of intense emotional arousal, you should give him a good hard spanking. Whether you begin gently, almost teasingly, or start hard and heavy depends on your tastes and your submissive's. If you start off hard, the first few blows will probably break the spell with the shock of their pain. (Remember, the more excited he is, the more pain you can give him, but also that the longer the punishment, the lighter the individual blows should be.)

   While you are spanking, keep up a running commentary on the color, heat, and probable sting of his buttocks, asking occasionally if he is sorry he was such a disobedient boy. You may add that if he hadn't committed his crime (do be specific), even now you would be having a quiet evening, he would be playing games with his friends, or whatever, instead of being so thoroughly and childishly punished. But he has asked for this paddling, and you must, however reluctantly, provide what he so clearly needs.

- *Rebellion.* Under the combined spur of the pain and your remarks, he may rebel, putting his hands behind him to shield his bottom, trying to crawl off your lap, or otherwise showing that he won't take the punishment one second longer. As long as he doesn't use the safeword, you must quell this rebellion. Threaten him with a redoubled punishment unless he settles down to take his medicine like a good boy. You may have to tie his hands behind his back, strap him down to a table, or otherwise bind him before you go on.

- *Submission.* At some point he will stop struggling and accept his punishment. At this point he knows he was wrong and is willing to accept whatever chastisement you deem necessary. Start winding down the punishment now.

   After the chastisement is done, make sure he kisses the instrument of correction (refusal to do so means another walloping is in order) and thanks you sincerely for punishing his naughty bottom. Then you may stand him in a corner or make him perform any of the other additional penalties.

He may still be sexually aroused, in which case you may permit him to masturbate. Or he may have ejaculated while the punishment was happening, usually a signal to end the punishment. As always, some subs will not become sexually aroused during a scene; for them, the scene itself can be all the satisfaction they need.

- *Ultimately, Peace.* Having taken his punishment, the schoolboy feels renewed. He has been spanked and is the better for it. Do it again next week.

Enacting the Scene

Act Two is the heart of this fantasy, but you shouldn't neglect the three-act structure and just rush into spanking. A well-planned Act One makes a spanking all the juicier, while a good Act Three rounds off the experience.

Act One. The establishment of your authority may be very brief. You could begin by informing the lad what his crime is and what his punishment must be. Heighten suspense and anticipation by taking your time.

Act Two. Spank him!

Act Three. After the chastisement and any subsequent punishment, console your little darling. Show him that you love him, even though you will continue to apply your hairbrush to the seat of his problems whenever he is need of correction. Allow him to cry in your arms or to express his contrition in other ways. (Use your imagination.)

Variations on the Fantasy

The schoolboy may need to become an adult infant or a sissy maid after his spanking. Do please remember that his stages of correction are also applicable to the punishment of any other type of submissive. Have fun.

12

THE QUEEN:
Maid Service and Petticoat Punishment

If you were Queen of pleasure / And I were king of pain / We'd hunt down love together..." – Algernon Swinburne, "A Match"

The sissy maid happily serving his Queen, doing everything from scrubbing the floors to serving her tea to giving her hours of oral servitude, is a sight to gladden the heart of any right-thinking Dominatrix. His sweet little French maid's costume, complete with ruffled panties and multi-layered crinoline, perky cap and lacy apron, is the last word in Ladylike attire.

Although his costume may be ultra-Feminine, he is usually a male who lives a life so intensely masculine that he must make some sort of balance. He answers the need of his Feminine side by acting her out: dressing, walking, and acting like a Female; by obeying a Woman's commands; and especially by burying himself in the Shrine of Womanhood. The Chinese would say that he is soaking up the Yin essence from the sacred spot. The lucky Queen merely says that he is of all submissives the most adept and eager at oral servitude, and consequently the most fun to play with.

For the Mistress, the pleasures are manifest: service of a type few people can afford these days (for a sissy maid will act as housekeeper, Lady's maid, scrubWoman, and sexual plaything), plus a chance to practice complex and intricately scripted Dominance. The fantasy offers an amazing range of possibilities, from gentle and affectionate service to severely punitive ordeals. And the two ends of the spectrum can both be played out in the same discipline session.

It's no accident that the Queen fantasy is placed at the center of all the fantasies, for this archetype can comprise all the others. The sissy maid may combine elements from the adult infant, the schoolboy, the slave, and the votary. And the Queen had better live up to her title and become a Mistress of all the arts of Domination, from basic bondage and discipline to commanding worship.

The Elements of Fantasy

Many other fantasies can be played out with thrift-shop goodies and lots of imagination. But the best costumes, setting, and props are crucial to the success of the Queen fantasy. Your sissy maid longs for an escape from the drab, harsh male world, into the rich colors and silken textures of Femaleness. Weighed against the wonderful service he is offering you (and his undoubted loyalty, especially if you prove to be a skilled and inventive Mistress), even the high cost of a good maid's outfit, crinoline, and stockings shouldn't faze you. The script, too, should be rendered with care. A careful, painstaking maid deserves the best of all possible scripts. Otherwise, you might end up doing your housework by yourself again, cursing every broken nail.

The Script. Scripting the Queen fantasy depends in large part upon the needs of your sissy maid. Unfortunately, he is highly unlikely to tell you what they are. Why not? On one level, he wants only to please you. And that's what he will say, if you should try to ask him straightforwardly about his fantasy needs.

On a deeper lever, however, he wants you to know by instinct just what he longs for. Somehow, asking for what he wants spoils the experience. It sullies the purity of his service for you, and makes your Dominance just one more thing he is responsible for.

Luckily, lest you go mad wondering what this man in lace and ruffles wants and needs, you have another source of information. After years of experience, I can tell you in general what he desires. (Check the section on "The Needs of the Sissy Maid" for additional suggestions on how to determine any additional quirky desires.)

His first need – for Feminization – is discussed at length under "The Needs of the Sissy Maid."

His second need is for you to be happy and satisfied with his service. He doesn't just want you to Dominate him, but to want to Dominate him. He wants a Mistress to dream incessantly of Ruling him, one who will create new and wonderful scenarios in which he is your plaything or slave and you are a gleefully wicked Queen.

His third need is for real Dominance. He doesn't want to act out his own fantasy. He wants you to take charge – and advantage – of him. If you're as softhearted as he is, this can lead to an impasse, sometimes a tragic one. Brace yourself to be the Bitch; it is actually the only thing that will please him.

Figure out what household tasks you most detest, what small personal services you most enjoy, and then fashion your script around his performance of them. Some suggestions follow:

- *Hand laundry.* Sissy maids love washing and rinsing out panties, slips, and stockings. They will even press them dry with an iron, although this procedure is not advised for nylon undies.

- *Minor sewing and mending.* Some sissy maids are adept at embroidery, knitting, or other crafts for which you can take the credit. Others can be taught. Sending him to an evening sewing class may be advisable.

- *Any and all housework,* from scrubbing out the toilet to vacuuming the living room. No self-respecting or considerate Queen ever does housework except in an emergency.

- *Making and serving snacks, tea, or breakfast in bed.* "Tea" may be a single cup or a full-fledged meal complete with cookies and lace napkin. If your friends are in on your activities, the sissy maid will gladly serve you all, incidentally showing off your fine training and his total obedience.

- *Giving massages, facials, manicures, pedicures, or foot baths.* (See instructions for foot baths in Chapter 14.)

- *Brushing out your hair, helping you to dress, and anything else a hired Lady's maid would normally do, including polishing your shoes.*

- *Carefully shaving the Mistress's legs, armpits, and even pubic area, if the Queen desires.* (He should use a new blade, a great deal of gentleness, and lots and lots of lather.)

- *Acting as bath slave.* By all means take advantage of this delightful fetish! Few pleasures are more voluptuous than having a devoted sissy maid soaping and rinsing you, gently drying you, rubbing your flesh with perfumed lotions, and finally indulging you with body worship and oral servitude.

And these are only a few of the many delightful services available from a well-trained sissy maid.

In return, you offer him the Feminization he craves as well as a stern punishment or wicked ordeal to focus his sensations. Once you've chosen one or two services, you must also choose a torment to go along with it. The following suggestions may be of help:

- *A session of bondage and CBT*

- *Verbal humiliation, including teasing for his sissy desires*

- *Intensive interrogation about your submissive's sexual history, fantasies, practices, and most humiliating experiences*
- *A spanking, hairbrushing, strapping, or birching for his faults as a maid*
- *Physical humiliation, including water sports (see Chapter 13) or making him serve as a table or hassock for your feet*

Again, these are just a few suggestions for painful interludes in your script. You may also borrow any technique or practice from the other fantasies.

Costumes. Good costumes are essential to the Queen fantasy. You should be dressed in a way that pleases you: Queens wear anything from leather to nylon slips. (Although baggy sweats tend to be untantalizing, for some curious reason.) The sissy maid has a passion for underclothes, and you might do well just to wear bra and panties, or a slip and stockings.

But for once your costume is less important than your submissive's. He should be clad in the best maid's uniform you can afford, complete with stockings, corset, ruffled panties, ruffled crinoline, ruffled apron, and maid's cap. I doubt sincerely that you will find anything remotely acceptable at the local thrift shop. Unless one of you can sew, you'll have to purchase the outfit. And that can run into bucks. The only consolations are that sissy maids tend to earn a lot of money, and that you can buy the outfit one piece at a time. Making each new piece a reward for good behavior can be a tantalizing process in itself. Each new piece of clothing or equipment must be accompanied by an elaborate fantasy scenario. The whole outfit could keep you in scripts for months.

You can also start out by dressing him in genuine Ladies' lingerie. Slips, panties, girdles, corsets, and bras are generally favorites. Most sissy maids prefer candy pink to all other colors, and they love lace and frills. (They also love compression, so a corset is a real necessity for this submissive.) When you hand your sissy his new lingerie and command him to put it on, his frisson of embarrassment and arousal will give you quite a thrill.

As for shoes, if his feet are reasonably sized (men's 10 or less), you should be able to find Women's high heels to fit him. (The specialty houses for transvestites are outrageously expensive, but they do have sexy designs.) Open-toed styles are best. If you have ever suffered in spike heels to impress some male, this is your hour of revenge. Savor it.

Try not to get chintzy clothes. Your sissy maid needs to revel in sensuality: the luxurious texture of fine fabrics, the distinctive taste and scent of your Shrine, the intense stimulation of penis punishment.

Setting and Props. The setting and props should carry out the theme of lush, romantic sensuality. Try to furnish at least one room of your house with taste and perfection; Victorian style is best suited for this fantasy, as Colonial and modern are too severe. Buy a wicker bed tray for those maid-served breakfasts in bed. Make everything both of you see, taste, touch, hear, and smell utterly delightful to the senses. You should sink into a world of carnal voluptuousness.

The Skills of a Queen

Handling a sissy maid requires you to give commands for every least action, and there's a great deal of action in the fantasy. Serving you, cleaning your house, washing your panties, all may grow dull and unenticing for the submissive unless you think ahead and keep the fantasy flowing.

Your Dominance in this fantasy is nearly total, and you'll need a repertoire of useful skills to maintain control not only of your sissy's actions but also of his thoughts and feelings.

Verbal Humiliation. As we've noted before, verbal humiliation is more than just profane abuse. (That's so inelegant.) Subtle teasing and mockery is well-suited to most sissy maids, but verbal humiliation need not end with your laughing at how ridiculous he looks in drag, trying to appear Feminine when he's no more than a great, coarse male. Indeed, the best verbal humiliation may be the humiliating words he says himself. At your command, of course.

Renaming. I hope my attentive Readers have not forgotten all those useful suggestions in Chapters 5 and 6. You must rename your maid!

The Forced Confession. Do you suspect that he keeps sexual secrets, masturbates without permission, fantasizes about your friends and family, or commits other violations of your law? Try forcing a confession from your sissy maid.

This process should be done with the maid in bondage or perhaps kneeling; in some way he must be forced into a physical position that emphasizes his helplessness and your power. Then torment him physically – with punishments, discipline, nipple clamps, whatever – while you interrogate him thoroughly.

You may use a sweet, Feminine voice, or bark questions at him, depending on your personal style, but make sure you keep up the physical and psychological pressure. Soon the sissy will crack and confess his naughtiness, for which you must punish him thoroughly. Add additional torments for forcing you to question him, instead of voluntarily confessing.

This is, incidentally, one of the best ways to discover those quirky needs that are unique to your sissy maid alone.

The Mantra. The mantra is your submissive's repetition, over and over, of a fact he finds almost intolerably shameful. You must dictate the wording. Again, this should take place during painful stimulation; it also works exceedingly well when you are allowing your sissy maid to have an orgasm. Some sample mantras:

- *"I am Mistress Lorelei's panty slave."*
- *"I love Mistress Lorelei's panties."*
- *"I am a sissy who deserves to be whipped."*
- *"I want a panty cocktail. I need a panty cocktail."*
- *"Please torture me, Mistress Lorelei."*

Feel free to make up your own mantras. Focus on whatever most intensely arouses and embarrasses your submissive.

Scoring Systems. No, this isn't a sure-fire way for frat boys to get laid. (What kind of book do you think this is?) It's a system to classify and record all the potential merits and demerits your sissy maid could earn. Being judged is both seductive and shaming for the average sissy maid. (They also tend to be perfectionists unforgiving of their own faults and flaws.) If you keep score of those minor faults, weighed against his service, your sissy maid will be thrilled and blushing to hear how he's doing.

Of course, any room improperly cleaned, any service not performed to perfection, any fault of posture or failure of obedience, and you must make your maid redo the whole thing from scratch, in addition to suffering the usual penalties of discipline. Likewise, if he doesn't endure his punishments well, you should start over.

A few hints. Faults must be worth far more demerits than the submissive could ever possibly offset by serving well. Consequently, the submissive always owes you more service, deserves more punishment, and needs more training. (Punishment is one way to work off demerits; service, including rendering obeisance to your Shrine, is another but slower way.) He can never be allowed to get away with a positive score. Only when merits and demerits are even should he be permitted an orgasm. As harsh as this system sounds, he'll eat it up.

Physical Humiliation. Physical humiliation is not limited to punishment, although you may wish to discipline your sissy maid as you would any other submissive. Certain specific practices are effective ways to reinforce his identity as a maid while rendering him acutely embarrassed. Enjoy.

Panty Slavery. The panty slave has a thousand and one uses for your dirty panties, the riper the better. He wears them on his head, has them stuffed in his mouth as a gag, is forced to don them himself (if your sizes are compatible), and has to masturbate into them. He may also be forced to carry them one by one in his mouth to the bathroom sink, where he must hand-wash them, rinse them, iron them dry, fold them, and put them away, before he returns for the next pair.

Although the same tasks may be done with bras, girdles, slips, or stockings, panties have the most powerful charm, for they are in direct contact with your tantalizing Shrine.

The Panty Cocktail. This task is so special it must be dealt with by itself. To make a panty cocktail, ball a pair of strong-scented panties in your slave's mouth. Then slowly pour warm water, possibly spiked with a little urine of yours, into his mouth. (You may pour directly, although a large funnel held in his teeth can make the scene less messy.) The fluid will be filtered through the panties, picking up their taste, and your submissive will swallow it. Voila, a panty cocktail!

Furniture Imitations. Make your sissy maid kneel on the floor and act as a small table (set a few magazines or a flower vase on him) or as a footstool. If he's not perfectly still, smack him into line with a wooden paddle, complaining about having to fix the furniture.

Shaving Body Hair. Already covered in Chapter 8, but do try it on your sissy maid. His hairlessness is your badge of possession.

Maid Training. Force your maid to curtsy twenty times in a row, to walk in high heels with a book on his head, to do any of the other thousand embarrassing things that will train him to be a useful maid. Maid training can go on indefinitely, and you may return to certain skills at intervals to polish them up.

The Pleasures of a Queen

Having someone else do the housework – thoroughly, perfectly, at your command, while you relax and buff your nails – is such a common Female fantasy that it's not even kinky. But mere housework isn't the only satisfaction for the Queen. Detailed, lavish pampering combined with limitless power is undoubtedly erotic for many of us. And transforming a man into a painted, primping simulacrum of a Female can be extraordinarily liberating. Though it may make you re-examine exactly what masculine and Feminine qualities mean, it can also reassure you that no matter how much powder he wears, the central Female power that men envy is always yours.

The Needs of a Sissy Maid

A sissy maid needs control and discipline, as do all submissives, but mostly he needs to slip into a glittering world of Feminine sensuality and unmasculine passivity, where he has no responsibilities to think and choose, only to carry out your orders, and where punishment for any infraction is swift and certain.

The dynamic of this fantasy is fascinating. It really does crop up most often in males who work in almost exclusively masculine environments (sports, high-level government, engineering and computers, huge corporations, the armed forces). Although many of these employers have had to admit a few token Women over the years, they have not admitted any Feminine characteristics at all. They remain appallingly phallocentric (and therefore lopsided and ineffective, but that's neither here nor there).

And many of their brightest, most creative and far-seeing men – men who draw their brilliance from their mix of masculine and Feminine energies – feel so strained by the distortion of their natural equilibrium that they use this fantasy to restore their balance. The sissy maid is a male who so deeply honors Femaleness that he loves – and needs – to imitate it.

However, lest you worry that your husband is going to turn into a Girl and leave you with a best friend but no man, I should inform you that virtually no sissy maids are transsexuals. A man who dares express his Feminine side so openly is a man totally secure in his masculinity. When he's not being a sissy maid, he still has that deep appreciation of sensuality and that intense desire for cunnilingus, but he'll express it in vanilla sex of breathtaking skill and passion.

Individual Quirks. Your sissy maid may have needs I haven't mentioned. Perhaps he longs to incorporate some of the other fantasies into this one, or has a particular type of fantasy that he enjoys acting out. Snoop around, looking for the notebooks in which he pastes clippings, the magazines featuring his favorite type of Dominatrix, and any other evidence of his kinky desires. You may also try interrogation techniques, forced confessions, and so on. Also, try out different scenarios. You'll never know what will hit his hot buttons.

Forced Feminization. To counterbalance the desert of machismo in which the poor man daily swelters, he needs to refresh himself with a turn into Femininity. The more macho his environment, the more Feminine his reaction must be. A real Woman (unless she's a beauty contestant) can relax and not be a frosting-covered sweetheart all the time, but your sissy maid is likely to go all out, for the gooeyest possible version of Femininity.

Some of the Feminizing process your sissy maid welcomes may unpleasantly remind you of the good-Girl shackles you have learned to break. Remember, although you almost certainly had to rebel against being sweet, passive, and dependent, lest you choke on your own weakness, your submissive needs to learn these skills and qualities, lest he starve for affection and attention. You're both seeking balance, but in opposite directions.

Actually, the texts of how to be a good Girl and an obedient Wife – such as Marabel Morgan's nauseating "The Total Woman" or Helen B. Andelin's loathsome "Fascinating Womanhood" – can be read with profit by your sissy maid. (I hope they're out of print. Try a used bookstore.) Personally, I love the ironies involved. My marriage was indeed made happier by these Ladies' advice, but I was not the one who needed to abandon my personhood and submit in a swoon of ecstatic dependence. My strong, stalwart husband (the one with the macho job and the overwhelming responsibilities) was the one refreshed by temporarily dissolving into a puddle of sweet submissiveness. I hope Marabel and Helen are pleased. I know I am.

Feminine Clothing. Female clothing, especially lingerie, is drenched in the magical essences of Femininity. For the sissy maid, they symbolize not only their rightful owners, but also all the freedom, all the privileges he envies in Females.

Don't get huffy! (I hear you muttering about male privilege.) Despite centuries – millennia – of oppression, Women do have some advantages. We get to cry. We are allowed to be afraid, sad, protected, dependent, and spoiled in ways that little boys are never permitted. Little Girls are allowed to wear ruffles and lace (whether they want to or not), to dab on some of Mama's perfume, to play dress-up with Mama's makeup and clothing. If they have a brother, he may watch in anger and frustration as they enter this Female world, especially if his Sisters and Mother enjoy teasing and mocking him for wanting to join them in the fun. Do all little boys want to play dress-up? At first, before they learn that it's considered a sissy thing to do.

In short, Females don't have the terrible burden of maintaining masculinity at all times. We are freer to move in and out of sex roles. We have a wider range of expression and emotion, even before we become good Feminists and full human beings. Is it any wonder that sensitive, intelligent little boys should envy us that freedom and range? Or that the little boy mocked in the 1960s for being a sissy might become a shame-filled, curtsying sissy maid thirty years later?

For most submissives, Female dress is both a humiliation and a privilege. The sissy maid knows he doesn't deserve to wear the silken, ruffled garments of the superior sex, but he longs to taste their magic anyway. Consequently, just dressing him in Female clothing is erotic. Naturally, a chastity device is really needed under those layers of clothing, to make him feel more Feminine still.

Enacting the Scene

Your sissy maid tends to need longer, more elaborate scenes than some submissives. Your sense of power and control, and his of submission and shame, grow deeper every minute of a well-planned session.

Act One. Establish your authority by dressing him in garments of your choosing. You should then give him a list of commands (typewritten, by preference) and set him to the task or two you've chosen as suitable for today's session. Hover nearby, criticizing his performance of duties, noting down any flaws on your scoring sheet, and threatening dire consequences for his carelessness and clumsy masculine ways.

Act Two. Now is the time to make good on those threats. Whatever the punishment or ordeal you choose – and you may try spankings, CBT, bondage, or water sports, in addition to the specifically Queenlike acts of panty slavery, etc. – you should make certain he knows that his inadequate efforts to be Feminine have displeased you, and that you intend to train him as a thoroughly Feminine maid before long. He will be revealed to everyone as the sissy he is.

Act Three. After such intense punishment, many submissives would long for orgasm and consolation. Your sissy maid deserves a reward, too, but oral servitude is more in line with his – and your – real needs. After proving himself so well (or suffering such wicked punishment), the sissy maid should be allowed to serve you at length. Finally you may permit him to masturbate into your panties, perhaps while chanting a mantra of his panty slavery or while answering humiliating questions.

Variations on the Fantasy

The Queen fantasy is both domestic and savage, bridging the gap between the pleasant and tender relationship of a Nursemaid and her charge and the open, gleeful sadism of an Amazon with a captive. You may include scenes from any fantasy in your scenarios. Especially appropriate are the ordeals described at length in the Amazon chapter, the foot worship due a Goddess, and the diapering of an adult infant. Although some sissy maids enjoy extended schoolboy-type punishments, some do not. Remember, sissies are more aroused by shame and humiliation than straight pain. Any pain involved must be given a shameful dimension before it will stir his loins.

13

THE AMAZON:
Bondage, Discipline, and Humiliation

"She was an Amazon. Her whole life was spent riding at breakneck speed along the wilder shores of love." – Lesley Branch

If, before opening this book, you were asked to describe your mental image of a Dominatrix, you would probably have described an Amazon: skin-tight black leather corset, liberally studded in steel and draped in chains; steeple-heeled thigh-high leather boots, perhaps equipped with spurs; carrying a whip in one long-nailed hand and a cigarette in an ivory holder in the other. You might have added other popular perceptions: that the slim, leggy Female clad in leather and steel is a tall, blonde, highly paid prostitute.

That's an Amazon, all right. *An* Amazon, not *the* Amazon.

To take the last image first, very few Mistresses are prostitutes; even the Female Dominants who are professionals do not allow their clients to have sex with them. They offer a highly specialized service for which they are well paid, and they don't need to sell "plain vanilla" sex.

Then, the Amazon, amateur or professional, may be a tall, leggy blonde, or she could be a dumpy brunette or a positively Rubenesque redhead. You don't have to stand six feet tall and weigh 120 pounds to be a happy and effective Amazon. Finally, you don't have to wear enough chains to give you a dowager's hump or enough leather to reupholster a couch and chair. If this fantasy appeals to you, don't shy away from it on the grounds that you don't fit the image, you hate high heels, or you haven't got the cash to dress in leather head-to-toe.

Remember, *you* are in charge. This is Female Dominance, not Madison Avenue Dominance. You can dress as you please, look like yourself, and still enjoy your natural position of authority. Of course, many Women love the sensual look and feel and smell of fine leather (I do myself, though I prefer cinnamon suede with bronze or copper to the traditional black leather and steel). Some Amazons enjoy wearing six-inch heels; I loathe them, but I don't expect everyone to agree with me. If a Dominatrix can't be an individual, what Woman can be?

This fantasy may be enhanced by the proper costumes and props, but you get to decide what these are. For there is no single Amazon fantasy, just as there is no single way to be a Queen or a Nursemaid. The Amazon is not defined by figure type but by a certain kind of power relationship between Mistress and slave.

What is that relationship? It is a contest of wills, for in this fantasy the submissive is a rebellious captive and nearly an equal to the Dominatrix. Playing an Amazon can be a wonderful experience, for it calls on all your reserves of energy, courage, fierceness, and will. Your submissive will enjoy it too, for he can keep his manhood and self-respect after being conquered by such a powerful Mistress. In fact, the more he esteems your power, the more self-respect he keeps! So respecting you is essential to his peace of mind.

The Elements of Fantasy

Given the basic dynamic – between a powerful Female and a male who is not quite her equal – the Amazon fantasy can work itself out in a thousand different ways. I've included a long list of suggestions for the two characters in the section entitled "Script," but you may be able to come up with a unique twist. The setting, props, and especially costumes will depend on the fantasy roles you choose.

The Script. The Amazon fantasy offers unparalleled opportunities to vary your scripts and make the fantasy personally satisfying. Who have you always wanted to be? What Heroine or Female Villain would you like to become? The list below is only a sample of the richness available. Let your imagination run wild!

The Mistress may be:

- *A secretary turning the tables on her evil boss (as in the movie "Nine to Five")*
- *A Female pirate terrorizing the captain of a ship she has seized*
- *A pagan Ruler evaluating a prisoner of war's potential as a sexual plaything*
- *Catherine the Great of Russia doing ditto*
- *A cowgirl roping an obnoxious male colleague and taking him down a peg*
- *An Indian Princess taking revenge on an exploitive white settler*
- *A Female Revolutionary tormenting her male hostage (naturally, he's a spoiled member of the corrupt ruling party)*

- *A Nurse handling an obstreperous patient*
- *A Warrior Queen grilling a captive spy*
- *A Space Alien testing human male sexual response*
- *A Courtesan (in any time period from Ancient Greece to today) teaching an inconsiderate lover the proper way to treat Females*
- *A Wife punishing a neglectful or unfaithful husband*
- *A Tenant instructing a landlord on the negative consequences of sexual harassment and no heat*
- *A Sister teaching her brother not to be a Peeping Tom* (can also be done as cousins, neighbors, schoolfellows)
- *A Female Knight persuading fellow-soldier not to reveal her gender* (may also work with wars in other times)
- *An Abbess tormenting a wicked monk*
- *A Female Warden guarding a prisoner*
- *A Witch interrogating a judge who persecutes Witches*
- *A Sultana punishing the male who has dared to invade her harem*
- *A Victorian belle teaching a would-be seducer to respect Ladies*
- *A Lady Wrestler proving her superiority over her male rival*
- *A leather-clad Dominatrix, complete with studs and chains and spike-heeled boots, teasing and tormenting her love slave*
- *Wonder Woman or Tank Girl and a miscreant*
- *An Author getting revenge on an editor, reviewer, or plagiarist*

From this partial list, you can see that the Amazon fantasy offers a wide range of roles for both Domme and submissive. The only fantasy I advise against is the one in which the male submissive plays a rapist being caught and tortured by his victim; the danger here is not that he might decide to commit a real rape but that you could be overwhelmed with fury, lose the sense of erotic play, and really hurt him. On the other hand, that may be just the fantasy to turn on you and your love slave. The decision is yours; after all, you're the Mistress.

Costumes. Given the spectrum of possible fantasy roles, you could dress in anything from a harem outfit to an Armani suit, and your submissive's clothing range is just as wide. All I can say about costumes is that they should fit the fantasy and they needn't cost the earth. Yard sales and thrift shops offer all kinds of goodies. So do costume shops; every big city has them, and they sell or rent a wide variety of clothing. Watch for spring sales, when they clean out their old stock; you could get great clothes for very little. You can always use your imagination and whatever craft skills you possess to adapt, decorate, or create gorgeous outfits for you both.

But there is still one special segment of costuming that is significant in Female Dominance games. No, not leather.

Shoes and Boots. Of all the symbols of Female Dominance, spike-heeled leather shoes (or boots) are probably the single most powerfully evocative of the Feminine Regime. The high heels add to a Woman's height, slim and elongate her legs, and change her stride into a swaying, mincing amble exceedingly provocative to males. And additional details may also be seductive. Lace-up boots imply bondage and corsets. Tight black leather, vinyl, or latex not only outline and enhance the curves of the leg, the materials themselves are connected with erotic games. Dark, shiny, clinging materials form a sort of superskin, suggesting all kinds of wicked delights within – and if genuine leather is used, the aroma alone is alluring.

Even off the Female foot, a Woman's high-heeled shoes (or boots) are instantly recognizable as fetishes or sexual icons. They are so different in shape, size, cut, and color from a male's utilitarian oxfords that they naturally evoke Femininity in its most extreme form. They become a fetish, an object that displaces a person as a focus for sexual fantasy. And like all fetish items, shoes or boots first remind the fetishist of the Female he desires, then embody the excitement, and finally become arousing on their own.

Although fetishes can be developed for many items of Female attire – from the quaint Victorian passion for gloves or handkerchiefs to the modern lust for panties, slips, and corsets – shoes are virtually the only form of outerwear that has attracted much sexual attention. The reasons seem clear enough. A Woman's shoes (at least the fetish variety) are decorative, not utilitarian. (Has anyone developed an unconquerable passion for battered, mud-stained sneakers? Possibly one or two imaginative males. But most go for shiny spike-heeled pumps.)

Even the shape is inherently lascivious; seen from above, a Woman's shoe is remarkably suggestive of the Female genitalia. For centuries shoes have been recognized as a symbol for the Lady's Shrine. Remember the tiny, tight-fitting glass slipper in Cinderella? How about the young ladies who danced all night, wearing out their shoes, in the Hans Christian Andersen story, "The Red Shoes"? Or the shot of the snake slithering through an open-toed shoe in *Raiders of the Lost Ark?*

Given the tantalizing possibilities of shoes and boots, the Mistress's selection of footwear can be crucial. Some Amazons – wealthy or professional – pay thousands of dollars for custom-made, thigh-high, spike-heeled black leather boots that fit like a second skin. Other Mistresses wear less expensive vinyl boots, and still others prefer high-heeled shoes. If you love shoes, this is a wonderful fantasy for you. If you don't – and I admit to being a Domme who really prefers to work barefoot or in sneakers – you can still be an Amazon anyway.

Setting and Props. Having chosen a script, a costume, and (if you like) some lascivious footwear, you need to consider the setting and props best suited for your fantasies.

The Amazon's most common setting is called a dungeon. You needn't live in a half-ruined Gothic castle to play Amazon games, however, or even to furnish a well-equipped dungeon. Imagination and some basic purchases can go a long way toward converting your classic fifties ranch house into the lair of a Female Pirate, the harem of an outraged Sultana, or the bedroom of Catherine the Great. Most people seriously involved in Dominance games convert a spare bedroom or part of the basement into a playroom. Aside from the bondage gear described in Chapter 8, you should have eyebolts screwed into the walls at the level of your submissive's ankles, knees, waist, and outstretched hands, so you can chain him to the wall. A sturdy straight chair is useful for seated bondage and over-the-knee spankings. A four-poster bed is nice to have.

I could fill a book with optional equipment, but here are a few specific suggestions:

- *atmospheric lighting, ranging from red spotlights to oil lamps* (well out of the way of the lash)
- *a padded horse for whippings, canings, and birchings*
- *a set of homemade stocks*
- *a long, low couch or bench*
- *a massage table or a gym-style slantboard*
- *a sling* (attached to sturdy joists only; you don't want the ceiling to come down!)

Although this equipment can be fun, allowing you to play out many fantasies and perform various types of bondage and discipline, it's also unnecessary. You would do better to start simply, with the basic suggestions, and save the more athletic and expensive equipment for later, when you're sure what you will need and want. A basement crammed with costly black leather is no substitute for a vivid imagination and a lively sex drive.

The same goes for props. Aside from the basic disciplinary equipment that you must have (see Chapter 8), most high-priced props are unnecessary. By all means, choose the pieces that best enhance the atmosphere you want to create.

Smoky incense, along with an exotically patterned sheet thrown over the bed, can turn any room into a harem. But for your harem fantasy, you need not buy a thousand-dollar carpet, a six-foot brass water pipe, and an eighteenth-century divan.

Although authentic props are fun, they can also be expensive. Watch for thrift-shop goodies that can be adapted to several different fantasies. If you have one or two favorite fantasies that you play out often, you can collect specific props that seem appropriate. And, in fact, many Mistresses possess no more props than the basic bondage and discipline equipment.

The Skills of an Amazon

Perhaps more than any other archetype, the Amazon uses bondage to work her will. Study Chapter 8 with care and attention. You'll need to understand how to get a male tied up and how long you may keep him in one position.

As to what to do with him while he's in your clutches, you may borrow activities from the other archetypes, or you may exploit the special power relationship of the Amazon and her slave. These may be expressed in the specific set of activities called water sports – which you may or may not want to perform – as well as in two kinds of discipline: punishment and ordeal.

Water Sports. Half my Readers are probably saying "Goody!" while the rest are saying "Gross!" to the idea of playing with urine. No one will make you produce golden showers if the thought grosses you out of existence. (You are, after all, the Mistress.) If you're freaked, you may skip this section and go on to "Punishment and Ordeal."

But you may be curious or aroused by the thought of water sports, and in any case I grant you the freedom to make your own choices. Whether you play piss games or not, you have a right to know about them. Anyway, if you read the Queen chapter, you've already encountered a watered-down version of this in the panty cocktail.

Urine is a taboo substance and therefore one possessing great power to shame, thrill, excite, and subjugate your slave. It is associated in almost everyone's unconscious mind with those confusing days of potty training; with modesty, shyness, early sexual explorations of "down there," vaguely or specifically sexual feelings, and sometimes with pain and fear; and with issues of pleasure versus discipline, pleasing Mama versus pleasing yourself, the social order versus the individual.

That's a hell of a lot of freight for a simple bodily function to carry. And for males the act is even more specifically sexual; lacking our superior equipment, they must urinate with their sex organ, an overworked cylinder that also expresses their social and job status (haven't you heard men bragging and trying to top one another in the status game they themselves call "measuring dicks"?). Slang terms for the penis also are synonyms for an unpleasant person (prick, putz, schmuck) or an idiot (dork, dick, lobcock). No wonder they enjoy water sports. It's easier to stand in a golden shower than think about the implications of having two balls and a penis that may or may not stand up when you want it to.

The first thing you need to know is that human urine is sterile or nearly so, unless you happen to have hepatitis or a bladder infection. It won't poison you or your submissive. You can drink it or splash it around without causing hairy palms, birth defects, freezer burn, or anything except possibly a little psychosomatic nausea if your slave is squeamish.

On the other hand, it is wet and sometimes aromatic, it can water-stain carpets and upholstery fabrics, and it's messy. So you might want to limit your water sports to the bathroom, an easily mopped rec room or basement, or the great outdoors. Piss play on a white velvet couch is probably a bad idea. Using a child's plastic pool is both cheap and easy to clean up.

If you plan to try out water sports, do discuss them with your submissive beforehand. He may not be turned on at all, and he does deserve a vote, even if it's not the deciding vote. If you agree to try, you should prepare yourself by drinking lots of water earlier in the day. Caffeinated beverages act as a diuretic. So does beer, but you should never combine alcohol or drugs with Dominance play.

What can you do with golden showers? You can force your slave to kneel in the tub while you stand over him and spray him with your water straight from the source. You can bind him and hold a champagne glass to his lips, brimming with your urine (or even containing just a sip of it) and force him into drinking it, either as a punishment or as an ordeal. You can make him kneel while you piss straight into his mouth or into a funnel held in his lips.

All the suggestions so far involve you providing the golden fluid, but you can also force him to wet himself, to drink his own urine, or even to wash himself in it. You may want to force him to drink a great deal of water or coffee, or you can even tell him he has PMS and make him take Midol, which is both humiliating and effective.

Punishment and Ordeal. Both punishment and ordeal make use of the same repertoire of restraints, smacks, lashes, pinches, cock tortures, verbal humiliation, and physical humiliation. The difference between them is the purpose of the pain.

Although the discussion that follows offers various differences between the two activities, remember that in the real world (which includes acted-out fantasies, rather than those left as dreams), few things are pure and simple. Most punishments include a hint of the ordeal, and most ordeals also serve some of the purposes of punishments. The guidelines below are designed to help you understand how to plot and script your sessions and what specific things you can do for your own pleasure and the benefit of your submissive.

Punishment exists to break a submissive male's resistance, so that he humbles himself before you in a agonizing ecstasy of submission. To that end, you use the intense stimulations of pain, humiliation, and terror to propel him beyond his workaday self – controlled, reserved, and unemotional – through the walls of conventional masculinity and into a world where he can feel and be, where he can expiate his sins and safely experience the terror he would ordinarily hide from.

In punishment, the pain is a means to an end: it helps him "burst into that silent sea" and finally, if only for an hour, feel. It purges his guilt – guilt he may never let himself experience in ordinary life. For punishment to be effective, you must breach his defenses. In other words, the result you desire is his total capitulation. Only then can he be free and at peace.

Ordeal is somewhat different. Using those same intense forms of stimulation – pain, humiliation, and terror – the ordeal strengthens a submissive male's defenses, makes him surer of his masculinity, proves his worthiness. He still feels the pain and shame deeply, right down to the bone, faces them and conquers them and proves his endurance. The ordeal may be designed to prove his devotion to you or to test his manhood.

The pain of an ordeal – and there is usually considerable pain involved – is not designed to break through the slave's barriers but to test him, to show just what he can bear. For an ordeal to be effective, you must inform your submissive what torments he will be facing (a step which adds fear and suspense, but also gives a specific goal or benchmark for him to strive for) and you must make him believe that the goal is beyond the endurance of most men. Only having proved himself in a trial by fire will the slave be happy and at peace.

The Pleasures of an Amazon

The Amazon fantasy, probably the best-known image of the Mistress, is also the place where Domestic Discipline comes closest to the traditional Leather community. A good many Leatherwomen could classify themselves as Amazons, if they cared to, but they need not act out any of the roleplaying scenarios that are at the heart of Domestic Discipline. They simply enjoy flogging for its own sake – not as punishment, real or feigned, but as pure sensation. Their play partners don't pretend to be captive slave boys; they are men who want to surrender to a Woman, or who even prefer to get the sensation of a scene without submitting at all.

Given the freedom from scripts and expectations, the Amazon and the Leatherwoman can enjoy the blissful spontaneity of doing exactly what she likes with a willing partner who is willing to follow her lead into the darkest jungles of pain, pleasure, and desire.

Even if you are more comfortable with the roleplaying approach of Domestic Discipline, you can find wonderful freedom in being an Amazon, as well as the exhilaration of exercising sensual power over a willing submissive.

The Needs of a Slave

In this section, I have tried to draw a distinction between submissive males who need punishment and those who need an ordeal. But remember that these are rough guidelines, that a man's needs change depending on mood and circumstance, and that the two categories most often overlap.

The Slave Who Should Be Punished. To make a broad generalization, the submissive man who needs (or prefers) punishment has usually locked away his Feminine side almost completely. He tends to deny that he has problems of any sort, and may not be adept at discussing emotional issues. He may be uncomfortable with and deeply shamed by any form of Feminization. And he may not be especially pro-Feminist outside his Female Dominance fantasies.

He is most likely to enjoy the Nursemaid and Governess fantasies and the rougher end of the Amazon and Goddess fantasies, especially those practices designed to have a great deal of humiliation attached. He may clamor for intense birchings or lengthy spankings, for water-sports, or for boot worship. He may have some secret guilt about sex that is absolved by pain and Female Dominance.

The Slave Who Should Be Put Through an Ordeal. To make a broad generalization, the submissive man who needs (or prefers) ordeal is usually well in touch with his Feminine side, though at some wordless level, he may feel a bit ashamed of his own Feminine components, because none of the other guys seems to be troubled with, well, you know, feelings. Although in public he may seem pleasantly extroverted and one of the guys, he secretly tends toward self-doubt and introspection. With a Woman he loves he will usually be openly affectionate and emotional. He may long for Feminization, feeling it both an honor and a humiliation. He is more likely to identify himself as a Feminist outside his Female Dominance fantasies.

He is most likely to enjoy the Queen and Goddess fantasies, sometimes the Nursemaid fantasy, and the more egalitarian Amazon fantasies. He may love Feminization and is your best bet for truly lengthy and voluptuous foot worship and oral servitude, both vaginal and anal. He loves, honors, and respects the Feminine, and simply needs to have his own maleness tested by pain.

Or, quite frankly, he may just love sensation play for its own sake. It feels good. Even the pain feels good. And he needs it, wants it, and is willing to do almost anything to get it.

Enacting the Scene

The structure of the Amazon fantasy follows the classical three-act structure with gorgeous fidelity. The only real variation is whether you choose to fill Act Two with an ordeal or with punishment. However, given the wealth of possible roles for both of you, you could play out this fantasy twice a week for twenty years without repeating a script. (By the way, you should save your scripts and notes in a safe place! You never know when you might need one.)

Act One. The script itself naturally depends upon the fantasy character you're playing. You may wish to act out the whole scenario (from capture on), or start with a bound and helpless male. In either case, you have to let him know who you are (and who he is, incidentally), why he is under your control, what you ultimately plan to do with him, and what sufferings he is likely to undergo on his way to that denouement.

Then bind him in a helpless position (preferably one suitable to the script) and either prove that you are in charge (by demanding oral servitude, boot worship, or what you will) or proceed to the punishment or ordeal of Act Two.

Act Two. Now you must apply whatever disciplinary measures seem most efficacious. If you are testing your slave through an ordeal, explain what privileges he will be allowed if he comes through the trial by fire without whimpering or moving (or whatever you have decided). Also advise him on the awful penalties you will exact if he fails to endure.

If you are punishing a slave, inform him of his sins and transgressions and let him know whether you want to hear him cry out in pain. You need not inform him of the consolations in store when he has been thoroughly punished.

Whether you're inflicting punishment or designing an ordeal, you should consider bondage, verbal humiliation, and CBT, perhaps followed by a flogging. You may end up with water sports of some sort. You could also borrow the Queen's panty cocktail or the Goddess's boot or foot worship.

Whatever you choose, choreograph it carefully, so as to keep your slave's suspense rising and his body fully stimulated.

Act Three. Having endured punishment or an ordeal, your slave may need to be consoled or to demonstrate his new devotion to you. You may demand extended oral servitude (a privilege for which your slave may have suffered his ordeal), or you may allow him to reach orgasm by masturbation.

You may decide instead to have ordinary intercourse with him, especially if his ordeal was designed to test whether he was worthy to mate with you. Provided he passed the test, I see no objection to your binding him to the bed, mounting him, and providing you both with pleasure. This is your scene, and you can do anything you like with him, as long as it's safe, sane, and consensual.

Variations on the Fantasy

The Amazon fantasy may be readily adapted by bringing in elements from any of the other fantasies. As part of the punishment or ordeal, you may treat your slave as an infant, a schoolboy, or a sissy maid. You may demand the lengthy worship suitable to a Goddess.

You may also export Amazonian actions and attitudes, especially to the Queen and Goddess fantasies. If your submissive is an adult infant or a schoolboy at heart, however, he is unlikely to enjoy the heavy bondage that is so distinctively Amazonian.

14

THE GODDESS:
Keeping a Worshipper at Your Feet

"Drunk with fire, toward Heaven advancing, Goddess, to thy shrine we come." – Friedrich von Schiller, "Ode to Joy"

The Goddess fantasy can be extraordinarily satisfying to both the Dominatrix and her slave. She receives a great deal of loving touch and sexual worship; he has the pleasure of extended touching of a superior Female, as well as the acknowledgment of his own unworthiness. Pain may not even be involved, although some ritual punishment or trial by fire (not usually literal, of course!) may well be part of the scenario.

This fantasy also has Victorian echoes: the exalted Female, the abject male eager to touch even her glove or boot. Our ancestors much better than we that Femaleness itself is precious, a treasured ideal to which the male aspires.

The Goddess fantasy also offers a Dominatrix a taste of transcendent power. For many Ladies, this fantasy is merely a pleasant game, a way to receive the personal respect and tender ministrations due a Goddess. They don't take the spiritual ramifications seriously, but they enjoy the exotic atmosphere and the slave's devotion.

For some Goddesses, however, the sexual rituals are an erotic way to make contact with the Triple Goddess, the ancient Maiden/Mother/Crone who ruled our hearts before the male gods of the patriarchy were ever thought of. All the Triple Goddesses (and she appears in many ancient cultures) possessed and ruled a male consort, whom she used sexually and sometimes discarded. The Triple (or Great) Goddess demands reverence toward Women, respect and acceptance for sexuality, and harmony between humans and the earth they live on. As the representative of the Divine Feminine, the Mistress accepts the adoration and worship of a male votary or slave.

The Dominatrix who expresses her religious beliefs by becoming the High Priestess of the Goddess is really outside the scope of this book. (Although some Readers may be High Priestesses seeking new ideas, most Goddess worshippers already understand the basic dynamics of Female Dominance and male submission, and do not need me to explain their sacred myths.)

So this chapter is written under the assumption that you are designing rituals for your own sexual pleasure and that of your male submissive. It is perfectly possible to play out a Goddess fantasy without believing in the Triple Goddess; even the psychological aspects of the fantasy, in which a male seeks to balance his life by getting in touch with the Female anima within him, are unnecessary to sexual satisfaction. All you really need to enjoy this fantasy is provided below: a basic understanding of the elements, of the dynamics of power between the Goddess and her slave, and of various interesting erotic activities that can take place.

The Elements of Fantasy

The key to enacting this fantasy is worship. Don't imagine hymn-singing and lengthy sermons. "Worship" here has a specific meaning: the expression of adoration and respect by stroking, licking, and caressing the body of the Goddess. This sense of worship is expressed in the Episcopal wedding service: "with my body I thee worship." Yet you don't wish the body worship to degenerate to mere foreplay, a means to an end. The chance to touch your feet must be sufficient privilege to thrill your submissive.

Preserving a Goddess's emotional remoteness while enjoying your slave's ministrations is an entertaining trick and can be the source of years of pleasure. Creating an appropriate script and setting is vital to maintaining the illusion that you are divine.

The Script. The script can be simple (your slave wishes to offer you worship) or lengthy and complex (your votary desires a favor, but first must endure a lengthy ordeal to prove his worthiness or cleanse him from his transgressions). To design a script satisfying to both of you, you must balance the sensual elements of body worship with the other possibilities of verbal humiliations, physical punishment, Feminization, or whatever else is part of your ceremonies. Some slaves of the Goddess need a great deal of torment to cleanse them of sin or prove their manhood. Others prefer to spend hours massaging the feet of the Goddess, rendering obeisance to her Female Shrine, or serving her in other ways.

Consider your needs and those of your votary before you decide on the details of the script.

The script itself should be reasonably specific about such details as your identity and culture. You may choose to be a modern Goddess, so you can skip getting special costumes, settings, and props. In that case, your Femaleness itself is what deserves worship and attention, and you may dress in whatever way best enhances it.

But I think it's more amusing to be an ancient Goddess of some kind. Do a little research on the ancient Greek and Roman Goddesses and decide whether you wish to be the sensual Aphrodite or the savage and untouched Artemis. (The book *Goddesses in Everywoman*, by Jean Shinoda Bolen, is useful for this as well as having profound psychological insights.) Or you could look further and become an incarnation of the Triple Goddess in any of a number of cultures: Egyptian, Phoenician, Irish, Nordic, Welsh, or pure pagan. Would you rather dress like Cleopatra? Choose to be Isis or Astarte. Do you long to be a warrior maiden? Try being a Valkyrie. Does a medieval look appeal to you? Try one of the ancient Celtic goddesses, Welsh or Irish. You could be Ceridwen, Olwen, even the human heroine Boadicea (although she's a few centuries earlier than the Middle Ages).

The point in choosing an identity is not to force you into improving your education, but to make the fantasy vivid and specific. The Egyptian style appropriate to a scene featuring Isis would be all wrong for a Valkyrie. Choose what you like, and make it live in your fantasies. And if you simply can't decide between Artemis and Astarte, well, you can be both at different times. Some of the props and costumes can be used for several different Goddesses. Just be sure you make it clear to your slave just whom he is supposed to be honoring today.

Costumes. For Dommes who want to dress as a Goddess, the most commonly worn costume consists of a draped Grecian gown, made at home or adapted from a nightgown. Snake bracelets, sandals, and a small flogger or other multi-thonged whip complete the look. Vaguely medieval garb is also popular, as are caftans, cloaks, or, for the truly savage Goddess, short dresses made of fluttering scraps of suede or leather. In fact, whatever attire you find most impressive, erotic, and comfortable is suitable wear for the Goddess within you.

Some modern Goddesses wear the Amazonian outfit of sky-high heels and silver-studded black leather, but I myself find this puzzling. What's the point of being divine if you have to wear something uncomfortable? If you wear chains, they should be delicate and golden, not ones that look like you swiped them from the neighborhood motorcycle mama.

Your votary should dress as you dictate. A simple loincloth (or nothing at all) is most appropriate for a bath slave. Many Goddesses prefer to see their slaves garbed in no more than a collar and a cock restraint.

For certain rituals, however, Feminine garb best suits the votary. You may decree that he is forbidden to touch certain parts of your body unless he is wearing Female panties, for example, or you may demand that he dress in full drag to perform certain rituals. (For his temerity in donning Female attire, you must punish him thoroughly, of course. Yes, even though you commanded him to. That's part of the fun.)

Setting And Props. To choose setting and props, you should first consider the total effect of your fantasy. The modern Goddess may choose a conventional dungeon setup (as described in the Amazon chapter), or whatever other settings best suit her fantasy and occur to her imagination.

The other Goddesses must choose a setting appropriate to their personae. An outdoor scene is best suited to one of the nature Goddesses: Artemis or Demeter or the Triple Goddess. Clouds of incense, exotic music, and luxurious Oriental carpets evoke Isis and Astarte. Anything sensual and lush, especially hot baths, rich perfumes, and dim lighting, seems best for Aphrodite. Use your imagination.

You don't need to spend a fortune; you can often find props and even furniture at thrift shops. Or you can adapt things you already own. Few people escaped the sixties without at least one incense burner. Bring it out and light sandalwood incense to make the worship of Isis come to life. That nostalgic scent alone should make you feel nineteen again and ready for love.

The Skills of a Goddess

A Goddess may call on the skills of an Amazon, a Queen, a Governess, even a Nursemaid on occasion (if she's giving a ceremonial purge). She must be able to command a slave and punish him, dress him in Feminine garb, place him in bondage, verbally humiliate him, and even put him through the intense stimulation of penis punishment.

Yet the Goddess's distinctive skill is not bondage or discipline or humiliation, useful as these are to her. It is accepting worship. More even than the Queen, so lavishly served and honored, the Goddess exists to be touched, stroked, and stimulated. Orgasm is not the only purpose. Twenty minutes of foot massage may not give either party an orgasm, but it gives both of them an intense sensual pleasure. Although extended oral servitude does usually result in orgasm, often repeated and overwhelming climaxes, the contact is what really counts.

Your major need as a Goddess is to believe you deserve all the pleasure, all the touching, you will receive. Learn to demand it as a right. Get used to pleasure. Your Divine Femaleness is so unique and precious that your submissive will do literally anything to come in contact with it. When you realize that your Femaleness is a treasure that your slave is honored, even exalted, to be permitted to touch, then you will have the correct Goddess attitude.

Since your lowest part – in mystical terms, the part of your Holiness that actually connects with the lower world – is the foot, it is most appropriate for your submissive to approach and worship it. Moreover, the Female foot is a lovely and delicate member, exceedingly sensitive and all too often abused by uncomfortable shoes and other stresses and strains. Your votary should spend a good deal of time caring for your precious feet. You may demand foot baths, foot massage, or a combination of the two.

Foot Baths. This charming custom is both soothing and sensual. Moreover, it displays your slave in a very erotic and humbling position – kneeling at your feet – and is calculated to lead to more interesting activities.

Seat yourself in a comfortable chair, with your feet extended. Command your slave to bring in the equipment for a foot bath. (He'll probably have to arrange them on a large tray, which he may set on the floor as is. The towel should hang over his arm.) The equipment consists of the following:

- *A waterproof mat.* A small bathroom rug will do, or even a towel, in a pinch. Or you may simply use the tray, if it is large enough.

- *A basin filled with steaming, scented water.* Your slave should know the exact temperature you prefer, along with whatever bath oils, herbs, salts, or pearls you enjoy. If you like a plain foot bath, thin slices of lemon floating on the water are also a nice touch.

- *A sponge, washcloth, or small soft brush,* if you like them.

- *A bar of soap or tube of shower gel.* Don't stint yourself; these should be richly scented and emollient. Bath salts (or bubble bath) and soap with matching scents are a very agreeable luxury, and not outrageously expensive. Often you can get a set with coordinating lotion and talcum powder as well. If so, you may include these accessories on the tray for after the foot bath.

- *A second basin of plain hot water for rinsing.* (This is an extra luxury, not a necessity.) You may choose instead a thick washcloth wrung out in hot water.

- *A small plush towel for drying your feet.*

- *Pedicure equipment,* if you so desire.

After placing the basin on the mat, your votary should kneel at your feet and gently remove your shoes and stockings, if you are wearing them, and lift your feet into the water, Then, one foot at a time, he should gently wash, stroke, and rub each foot, using the sponge (or whatever) if that is your pleasure. Otherwise he should simply use his hands to work up a good lather, and rub them gently but firmly over each foot, drawing his fingers between your toes and taking care to rub your insteps and arches.

When your feet are lusciously clean and relaxed, the votary may rinse them in the second basin or wipe them with the hot damp washcloth. Then he should slowly and carefully dry your feet. If you wish, he may rub them with soothing lotion or talcum powder and proceed to a pedicure.

During this incredibly erotic process, you may be sitting back in your chair, relaxing. You may have candles lit, incense burning, music playing – whatever is to your taste. You may be sipping tea or nibbling grapes. The scene should stimulate all your senses and those of your slave, so that both of you are bathed in sweet eroticism.

Most important of all, you could be talking: telling your slave how obedient, privileged, or unworthy he is; retailing a fantasy adventure; talking about your Divine Femaleness; threatening future punishments; discussing the oral servitude to come; or whatever conversation strikes your fancy and fits your fantasy.

You may also, if you are a cruel Goddess, keep your votary mindful of your power by flicking him lazily with a crop or cat.

Once the feet are clean and dried, you may elect to receive a foot massage, a body massage, oral servitude, or any of a hundred other delightful services. Depending on your script, you may also proceed to punishing or rewarding your votary.

Variations on a Bath Theme. After experiencing even one foot bath, you may come to the conclusion that leaving such delight only to the feet is a bad idea, and extend the range to Shrine baths, hand baths, and whole-body baths. In each case the basic technique is the same – although you use a whole bathtub, preferably a Victorian slipper tub, for the whole-body bath.

Even a shower, for those deprived of a tub, may be enlivened by the use of a bath slave. Naturally, he'll have to get in with you, but you can hog the hot water with no feeling of guilt whatsoever. A multistream showerhead on a flexible hose adds immeasurably to the delight of this act.

Some Goddesses borrow an idea from the Queen and order their votaries to shave the Mistress's legs, armpits, and even pubic area.

More Games with Feet

Foot Worship and Massage. Foot massage may precede, follow, or preempt the foot bath. Some votaries find the scent and feel of sweaty feet more arousing than that of clean or perfumed feet. Allow him his little eccentricities; look what pleasures you can get from this man. The foot massage may be done barefoot or over stockings. Of all the many positions in which foot massage may be done, the favorite is to have the Mistress seated in a chair, her vassal kneeling at her feet. Massage should be tender, firm, and thorough.

Foot worship – a term often used for what might better be called boot worship – is the act of kissing, caressing, licking, and sucking the feet of the Goddess. For some lucky Women, few sexual acts feel better than having their toes luxuriously sucked. It ranks right up there with cunnilingus. You will never know until you try, and Female Dominance sessions are the ideal time to discover this hot new erogenous zone.

Boot Worship. Many of the Female Dominance magazines refer to this practice as "foot worship," although the sensation to the Mistress is hardly similar. Boot worship has less to do with the feet than the shoes or boots. Basically it consists of foot worship applied to the Mistress's footwear, an erotic displacement that many males find incredibly arousing. For the Lady involved, its erotic stimulus derives from the power involved in making a male bow down and lick her boots. (For more shoe symbolism, see Chapter 12, under "Costumes.")

Other Fetishes. Noting the extension of actual foot worship into boot worship, the intelligent Reader can see that the Female Divinity is expressed not only by the beautiful Female body but also on a Woman's intimate possessions. Even your clothing is saturated with your essence and therefore holy. The Goddess may choose to extend her power into various inanimate objects, which she commands her slave to worship. Panties, slips, gloves, stockings, and (of course) footwear are traditional; you may amuse yourself by making your votary worship other articles as well. The important qualities of the garment or possession are, first, its Feminine nature; second, its intimate contact with the Female Divinity; third, its ability to absorb the delicate perfumes of her body.

The Pleasures of a Goddess

The Goddess's pleasures are undeniably direct and sensual. Her power is, as always, a source of great satisfaction, but the lengthy touching and caressing she receives from her submissive is a central part of her pleasure.

The Needs of a Votary

The votary has the deepest respect and reverence for Feminine power. He knows that everything pertaining to Womanhood is suffused with erotic and spiritual force. Although the votary yearns to have the honor of contact with Female flesh, he would be happy simply to touch her boots, since this honor extends even to her possessions.

As a slave, he is willing to serve his Mistress unstintingly, to provide her with breathtaking and bountiful orgasms, and to undergo any ordeal she wishes. He may have to suffer from ritual cleansings, and he is also, of course, subject to the usual punishments for failing to please his Mistress.

Ordeals and Cleansing Rituals. The trial by fire or religious ordeal is a session of punishment, ranging from simple spanking to lengthy CBT. All the techniques should be familiar by now; what differs is the meaning of the ordeal. A submissive of any stripe is punished for naughtiness. A votary (or an Amazon's slave) endures an ordeal to prove his manhood. A Governess may wish to see her schoolboy's spirit break into obedience and submission. A Goddess or an Amazon wishes to test her slave for his worthiness – spiritual or sexual, respectively. If he breaks, he has proved himself unworthy.

The Goddess's ordeal is not much different than the one described in the chapter on Amazons. However, the Goddess may also insist upon cleansing rituals to purify her slave. They may be administered before he is permitted to touch her, after an absence, or after he has spent a session under the Rule of another Mistress.

Cleansing rituals usually include several forms of punishment, bondage, bathing, and sometimes golden showers and/or enemas. Plan them carefully to cleanse whatever part of your votary has been contaminated. For example, if he has been caught masturbating, focus the cleansing on his wicked fingers and penis. If he spent time with (or even fantasized about) another Mistress, the liberal application of a paddle, followed by a few strokes with the riding crop, should begin the process of purification, but you may also need to give him a panty cocktail (as described in the chapter on the Queen), an enema, and/or a golden shower to restore him to your complete Domination.

Only when all traces of the impurity are gone should you accept him back into your service. You may also choose to enact cleansing rituals on a weekly or monthly basis, just to keep him free of the taint of wicked thoughts.

Enacting the Scene

The classical three-act structure of a scene may apply rather loosely to the Goddess's domain. Some submissives are happy simply to serve and need little punishment. If you and your slave fit that pattern, concentrate on Act One, keep the punishment in Act Two to a minimum, and enjoy Act Three in whatever way strikes your fancy. Other votaries crave punishment, wish to undergo lengthy ordeals, or need frequent cleansing from impure thoughts. In that case, the establishment of authority in Act One may be brief, but the punishment of Act Two can be intense. In all cases, the release of Act Three should include plenty of Goddess worship of whatever type you most enjoy.

Remember, a happy Mistress is a sexually satisfied Mistress. No slave wants to fail by leaving his Goddess unfulfilled. Demand and get as many climaxes as you want.

Act One. The activities suitable to this stage of the scene should be familiar to readers who have been perusing this volume front-to-back. (If you have not, check the other fantasy chapters for suggestions.) Changing his clothes, placing him in bondage or in a penis restraint, showing him by voice and word that you are now his Goddess, you establish your absolute power and his absolute submission. You may wish to Feminize your slave, demand oral servitude, or receive foot worship. Depending on your script, you may find fault with the votary's performance (in which case, you proceed to Act Two and his punishment) or simply enjoy lots of stimulation.

If you Feminize you votary, it is not to punish him but to honor him with the touch of your Femaleness. He may be ashamed of his Feminine attire, but that shame is not merely the schoolboy's humiliation at being considered a sissy. It is a shame based in his knowledge of his own masculine unworthiness. You may follow Feminization with punishment for his temerity in dressing as the superior sex.

Act Two. Your slave must be punished, cleansed, or subjected to a trial by fire. You may use every technique from verbal humiliation to golden showers to make your point. If the purpose is to punish him, make sure he breaks into submission before you stop.

If, however, you are testing his devotion in an ordeal or purging his transgressions in a cleansing ritual, you can't go on until he breaks. In face, if he does break, he has failed. You have to know your male's sensitivities very well to do this properly, but it can be exceedingly satisfying if you do it right.

Tell him exactly what to expect – a dozen strokes of the cane, say, and ten minutes of penis punishment – and warn him about what behavior will constitute failure on his part. Be specific. A Governess can get away with saying, "I want you to take this like a man," because she fully expects her charge to take it like a little boy. But you are not punishing a naughty boy, you are testing the courage and devotion of a grown male vowed to your service, and you owe him a clear and complete description of what he must achieve to pass the endurance test. Say, "You must endure ten lashes without moving or crying out, or I will gag you with these wet panties."

Yes, you should use your descriptive powers to make the coming ordeal seem almost unbearable, but you may not lie. Say, "Each lash will burn like lightning against your naked skin. You will long to writhe and moan, but you know you must lie still and take whatever your cruel Goddess chooses to give you – yes, and thank me for my kindness in punishing you so severely!" Don't say, "I'm going to give you a thousand lashes," and then give him ten. Don't even promise a dozen and then give him ten. That isn't kindness. The votary needs to test himself against a known benchmark.

Act Three. Release! All the wonderful activities of Act One may be recapitulated here. Whatever reward you wish to offer for his manful fortitude through his trial by fire, whatever intimate rituals he may now perform since he has been cleansed of sin, or whatever activity he has just been punished for previously bungling, may be done to your satisfaction and his.

His satisfaction may be taken in a number of ways: masturbating in panties to offer his seed to the Goddess is quite popular, or you may snap on a vibrating cock ring and give him a hands-off orgasm, or you may condescend to rub his penis yourself, or mate with him in a ritual climax.

Variations on the Fantasy

This fantasy works best with the Queen or Amazon fantasies. You can readily combine the Goddess archetype with the feminization and service of the Queen fantasy or the ordeal and bondage of the Amazon.

If your submissive male prefers the Nursemaid or Governess fantasies, you may want to work out a trade-off. You will baby or chastise him to his heart's content, but only after he has earned it with a lengthy session of foot worship or whatever you please. Do not agree to postpone your pleasure until after his fantasy, unless you know absolutely that your man is honorable about such things. Remember, control the cock and you control the man – a pitiable but accurate assessment of most males' priorities and emotional development. Or you may agree to alternate between the two forms of fantasy.

TEN RULES

For a Successful Mistress

"The rule of joy and the law of duty seem to me all one." Oliver Wendell
Holmes, Jr.

1. Control the orgasm, and you control the male.

2. To make any fantasy work, you must build suspense in your submissive.

3. Stimulation plus frustration equals service and submission.

4. Every submissive will try to test the limits of your Rule. Never let him get away with anything. He needs you to be both firm and consistent.

5. Physical pain alone cannot satisfy a submissive. (A masochist, yes.)

6. The more aroused your submissive is, the more pain he can take.

7. The more effective your psychological Dominance, the less pain you will need to inflict to control and satisfy your submissive.

8. All punishment is a balance between intensity and duration. More intense pain should last less time; if you want to prolong the punishment, use less intense stimulation.

9. Submission increases with time. As long as you maintain firm control, the longer a session lasts, the more thoroughly submissive your male will become.

10. Your control and pleasure are inextricably intertwined with his submission and pleasure.

GLOSSARY
Of Female Dominance Terms

"The chief merit of language is clearness, and we know that nothing detracts from this so much as unfamiliar terms." – Galen

"Taffeta phrases, silken terms precise." – Shakespeare

Amazon. A Dominatrix who enjoys capturing and tormenting recalcitrant males. Very much like an ancient Amazon, she is a warrior and ruler.

authority. The natural power, belonging exclusively to Women, of Ruling, Reigning, choosing, and judging.

backboard. A padded wooden device fitted with straps, designed to correct the posture of a slovenly male.

birch. A bundle of birch branches, often kept in pickle, and used upon the misbehaving male's bare fundament. A disciplinary tool of great value when used judiciously.

buttocks. The proper locale for nearly all physical corrections, such as spanking, caning, whipping, birching, strapping, and paddling.

butt plug. A thick cone of leather or plastic, insinuated into a disobedient slave's anus to remind him of his lowly status.

cane. A long slim switch (originally made of rattan, now available in many materials) and used (especially in England) for the correction of particularly wicked and disobedient submissives. Use with extreme care upon a bare or clothed bottom.

chastity device. A leather, metal, or plastic device, usually fitted with locks, for the restraint of a submissive male's unruly member. It may make masturbation or even erection impossible.

chastise. To physically correct. Practiced upon a submissive male by his wise and kind Mistress, who wishes only to guide him into a more suitable way of life.

climax. To achieve orgasm. The Dominatrix may enjoy this experience as often as she pleases, but it tends to be demoralizing to the submissive. The Mistress must strictly limit his access to this supreme pleasure to ensure that it occurs only upon her command.

Clitoris. The holy and beautiful nubbin of Female flesh that is the mark and center of her authority and power. The only human organ designed for pleasure only, rather than utility.

clyster. An internal scrubbing useful for flushing the wickedness out of naughty young men.

cock. A male's unruliest member. To be teased, tormented, and tamed.

cock ring. A collar, often equipped with a leash, for the control of the male.

cock and ball torture; CBT. Severe genital punishment designed to put a male in his place.

corner time. After a chastisement, time the male must spend standing bare-bottomed in a corner, meditating on his sins.

cunnilingus. An act of worship at the Female Shrine. Demonstrates Feminine Superiority and male subservience.

diaper discipline. Placing a infantile adult male in a position emphasizing and punishing his childishness.

dildo. A rod-shaped instrument for controlling the male through his anus. Should have a flange at the bottom to prevent loss.

discipline. A necessary and delightful governance exerted by the Mistress upon the disobedient male. It can take the form of strict behavioral guidelines, control of dress and speech, verbal humiliation and scolding, and/or physical chastisement.

discipline session. An episode of Female Rule, emphasizing the Mistress's total control of the submissive male.

disobedience. Typical male behavior, to be curbed and punished by a wise Female hand.

Dominance name. The exalted and sublime title of the Mistress. To be spoken with reverence, fear, and respect.

Dominatrix. A Female who understands the relative value, virtue, and strength of Women and males.

enema. A thorough internal ablution of a naughty male's interior organs. Often undertaken to scour away masculine dirty thoughts by purifying both brain and bowel.

fantasy. A vision of perfect bliss, especially when it expresses Female Rule over naughty males.

Female. (In Domestic Discipline) The innately superior sex.

Feminine. Like a Woman. A term of the most superlative praise.

Feminization. The attempt of a male to become like a Female, through dress, speech, tone of voice, gesture, and action. "We must imitate the highest when we see it," Goethe.

foot worship. A demonstration by a humble male that even the lowest part of a Female's body is higher than he.

Goddess. A Mistress who allows mere males to rise from their low position by worshipping the glory of her Womanhood. She demands praise and devotion, and severely castigates those who deviate from her Rule.

Governess. A Mistress who expresses the superior moral position of Females by her tuition of the lowly adult male schoolboy. Such tuition generally consists of applied ethics – applied vigorously to the quivering, blushing nether cheeks of her charge.

hairbrush. An instrument for the taming of unruly locks and unruly buttocks. The bristles may also be used in the discipline of unruly cocks as well.

humiliation. A necessary element in the control of submissive males, it consists of informing him by word or deed of his own unworthy nature, or making him confess to his own shame.

Lady. Term of honor for any Mistress, but particularly in use for a Female who Rules one or several males who have sworn lifelong fealty to her service and person.

maid. A male who has undertaken to preserve his Mistress from disagreeable and dirty tasks, such as housework, in return for the rare privilege of serving and obeying her. A happy man.

male. The inferior sex.

Mistress. A Female who Dominates a male. A very high term of praise and glory for the Female who has discovered her own power and fulfilled her natural destiny.

naughty. Disobedient, misbehaving, possessed of uncontrolled impulses or wicked thoughts. Typically masculine, this condition can be cured or at least curbed by a thorough acquaintance with a Dominatrix of the proper stamp.

nipple clamp. A device for restraining and punishing the male by constantly reminding him of his higher Feminine side.

Nursemaid. A Mistress who specializes in handling the most recalcitrant and juvenile adult males, those who must be treated as infants or toddlers because they persist in acting like them.

obedience. The first duty a submissive male owes his Mistress; sadly, few males ever live up to this basic demand and therefore must be frequently disciplined.

oral servitude. A great honor for the submissive male: the chance to apply his ignoble mouth and perhaps tongue to the most precious part of his Lady's body.

ordeal. A test of worthiness, usually consisting of various taunts, torments, and titillations. The Queen, Amazon, and Goddess may all put a slave through these lengthy trials by fire to see if he is truly worthy of serving his Mistress.

paddle. A broad, flat wooden instrument useful for smacking mischievous bottoms. Best used when the culprit is bending over a school desk or chair.

pantaloons. Long drawers, often ruffled and lacy. Many wise Dommes use these to induce a sense of Female superiority in their sissy maids.

panty slave. A male submissive who can be controlled by Female items of clothing draped over his head, stuffed into his mouth, or worn on his own scorched sit-upon. May also refer to one who washes, irons, and cares for his Lady's lingerie.

penis punishment. Painful and humbling stimulation applied to a male's most uncivilized member. Discipline without damage is the goal.

power. The most notable Feminine attribute.

punishment. Appropriate treatment meted out to a submissive male by a just and prudent Dominatrix. The male must always respond with sincere expressions of gratitude and the invitation to repeat the chastisement whenever he requires it.

punishment writings. Written confessions to various misdeeds, useful for humbling the male and heightening his anticipation of punishment.

Queen. A Dominant Female who prefers to be served by a sissy male. She controls her submissives through shame, discipline, and especially Feminization.

Queening. A posture of triumph for a Dominatrix and blissful humiliation for the submissive, it consists of the Lady seating herself (clothed or nude) upon the face and lips of her grateful slave. On special occasions she may even permit him to render obeisance.

Reign. The Dominance of a Female, especially her power to control a male's thoughts and sensations for a lengthy period of time.

Regime. The Mistress's power to choose and command during a discipline session; used loosely of the session itself.

render obeisance. To salute the Female Shrine, sometimes even the Clitoris, with the lips and tongue. A rare and precious privilege for any vassal.

Rule. A Female's innate prerogative.

schoolboy. A submissive adult male who realizes that in his youth he did not sufficiently obey or attend to the Women in his life. He attempts to atone for his negligence by assuming a subservient role, accepting teaching and punishment from a powerful Female.

session. An all-too-brief episode of Female Dominance.

Shrine. A Woman's most secret place, beautiful, sweet, and worthy of worship.

sissy. A male who understands the superior value of Women and seeks to better himself by becoming like them.

sissy maid. A submissive lucky enough to serve a Queen by following her orders to dress and act as a Female. Commonly does her housework, worships at her Shrine, and fulfills her other desires. The happiest life for many males.

sissy panties. Ruffled panties worn by the male (usually a sissy maid) to signify his respect for the Female. His shame and humiliation at wearing them result from his knowledge that he is unworthy to don Female garments.

slave. A male who is possessed, controlled, and punished by a Female Dominant. Virtually synonymous with submissive, but most likely to have fantasies of the Amazon or Goddess archetype.

spanking. A childish punishment useful in controlling many males. Spankings may be administered over the knee, using hairbrush or hand, and ideally upon a bare pair of bottom-cheeks. Often followed by time in the corner.

strap; also **strop.** A leather belt or razor strop suitable for applying vigorously to the nether cheeks of the naughty male. Painful and humiliating, especially when the submissive has just been soaking in a bathtub.

strictness. One of the finest qualities of the Female Dominant.

submission name. The new name bestowed by the Mistress upon her submissive, which signifies his role as an inferior and his obedience to her.

submissive. An intelligent male who understands the proper relationship of the sexes. To be treated by the Dominant Female with consideration, affection, and total control.

switch. 1: A long, slim tree branch or twig, commonly taken from hickory, peach, or willow trees, to be used upon the buttocks of unruly males. 2: To change Dominance/submission roles.

Tyrant. A Woman who is in her rightful place: in command. To be feared, respected, and obeyed.

underling. Any male.

vassal. A male who has sworn to obey a Female Dominant and is thenceforth her property.

whipping. 1. A chastisement suitable for a submissive male who is behaving like a naughty schoolboy or a disobedient slave. Administered by the Mistress, using a leather cat, riding crop or singletail only on the upper back or the buttocks, this is a severe punishment, better used as a symbolic form of discipline. 2. Used loosely, any physical castigation.

Woman. A member of the superior sex. To be honored, reverenced, adored, and obeyed at all times.

Womanhood. Femaleness in all its glory. Also, the Female genitalia.

worship. To prove one's adoration of the Mistress by kissing, licking, and stroking a symbolic part of her body or her clothing, such as the feet, the Shrine, or the panties. Done only on command.

ABOUT THE AUTHOR

Lorelei is a polyamorous bisexual Domme with an occasional masochistic streak – a sexual and social identity that could be a full-time job if she weren't overscheduled already. When she isn't busy beating someone, she is a professional writer and editor. She has two cats, ten thousand books, and not nearly enough time to do what she likes.

BDSM/KINK

... But I Know What You Want: 25 Sex Tales for the Different
James Williams $13.95

The Compleat Spanker
Lady Green $12.95

Erotic Slavehood: A Miss Abernathy Omnibus
Christina Abernathy $15.95

Erotic Tickling
Michael Moran $13.95

Family Jewels: A Guide to Male Genital Play and Torment
Hardy Haberman $12.95

Flogging
Joseph W. Bean $12.95

The Human Pony: A Guide for Owners, Trainers and Admirers
Rebecca Wilcox $27.95

Intimate Invasions: The Ins and Outs of Erotic Enema Play
M.R. Strict $13.95

The Kinky Girl's Guide to Dating
Luna Grey $16.95

The New Bottoming Book
The New Topping Book
Dossie Easton & Janet W. Hardy $14.95 ea.

The (New and Improved) Loving Dominant
John and Libby Warren $16.95

Play Piercing
Deborah Addington $13.95

Radical Ecstasy: SM Journeys to Transcendence
Dossie Easton & Janet W. Hardy $16.95

The Seductive Art of Japanese Bondage
Midori, photographs by Craig Morey $27.95

The Sexually Dominant Woman: A Workbook for Nervous Beginners
Lady Green $11.95

SM 101: A Realistic Introduction
Jay Wiseman $24.95

21st Century Kinkycrafts
edited by Janet Hardy $19.95

GENERAL SEXUALITY

A Hand in the Bush: The Fine Art of Vaginal Fisting
Deborah Addington $13.95

Paying For It: A Guide By Sex Workers for Their Customers
edited by Greta Christina $13.95

Phone Sex: Oral Skills and Aural Thrills
Miranda Austin $15.95

Sex Disasters... And How to Survive Them
C. Moser, Ph.D., M.D. & Janet W. Hardy $16.95

Tricks... To Please a Man
Tricks... To Please a Woman
both by Jay Wiseman $13.95 ea.

When Someone You Love Is Kinky
Dossie Easton & Catherine A. Liszt $15.95

TOYBAG GUIDES:
A Workshop In A Book $9.95 each

Age Play, by Bridgett "Lee" Harrington

Canes and Caning, by Janet W. Hardy

Clips and Clamps, by Jack Rinella

Dungeon Emergencies & Supplies, by Jay Wiseman

Erotic Knifeplay, by Miranda Austin & Sam Atwood

Foot and Shoe Worship, by Midori

High-Tech Toys, by John Warren

Hot Wax and Temperature Play, by Spectrum

Medical Play, by Tempest

Greenery Press books are available from your favorite on-line or brick-and-mortar bookstore or erotic boutique, or direct from The Stockroom, www.stockroom.com, 1-800-755-TOYS.